200 mini cakes and bakes

hamlyn | **all color cookbook**

200 mini cakes and bakes

An Hachette UK Company
www.hachette.co.uk

First published in Great Britain in 2010 by Hamlyn
a division of Octopus Publishing Group Ltd, Endeavour
House, 189 Shaftesbury Avenue, London, WC2H 8JY
www.octopusbooksusa.com
Copyright © Octopus Publishing Group Ltd 2011

Distributed in the U.S. and Canada by Octopus Books
USA: c/o Hachette Book Group USA, 237 Park Avenue,
New York, NY 10017, USA

Some of the recipes in this book have previously
appeared in other books published by Hamlyn

ISBN 13: 978-0-600-62270-3

A CIP catalogue record for this book is available
from the British Library.

Printed and bound in China
10 9 8 7 6 5 4 3 2

Standard level spoon measurements are used in all recipes.

Ovens should be preheated to the specified temperature
– if using a fan-assisted oven, follow the manufacturer's
instructions for adjusting the time and temperature.

Fresh herbs should be used unless otherwise stated.
Medium eggs should be used unless otherwise stated.

The Food and Drug Administration advises that eggs
should not be consumed raw. This book contains some
dishes made with raw or lightly cooked eggs. It is prudent
for vulnerable people such as pregnant and nursing
mothers, invalids, the elderly, babies, and young children to
avoid uncooked or lightly cooked dishes made with eggs.
Once prepared, these dishes should be refrigerated and
used promptly.

This book includes dishes made with nuts and nut
derivatives. It is advisable for those with known allergic
reactions to nuts and nut derivatives and those who may
be potentially vulnerable to these allergies to avoid dishes
made with nuts and nut oils. It is also prudent to check the
labels of pre-prepared ingredients for the possible inclusion
of nut derivatives.

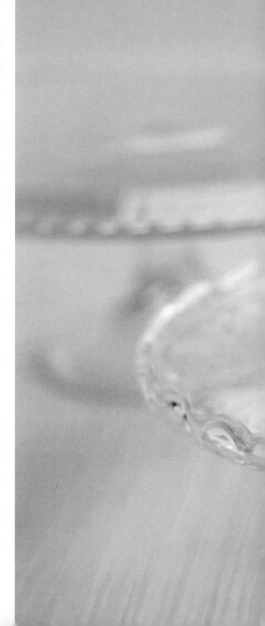

contents

introduction

introduction

Baking continues to maintain its appeal as a thoroughly rewarding form of cooking, and there are plenty of reasons why baking "mini" cakes has a particular appeal. We don't always want a great hunk of chocolate sponge cake or fruit pie but a small "taster" portion of a sweet morsel that's packed with flavor and is reassuringly and comfortingly sweet. Some of the cakes such as the muffins and simple cupcakes are quick to make, ideal for a family treat at any time of day, while others are more time consuming and best made for a special occasion. Because of their size, some of the bakes are intentionally richer and more flavor intensive than larger cakes, perfect for passing round after a special supper or at the end of a drinks and nibbles party. A selection of several mini cakes in contrasting flavors and textures makes a stunning display that'll attract plenty of appreciative tasters for this sort of entertaining. Manageable little morsels which are so easy to just pop in the mouth!

equipment

A glance around any large cook shop will reveal a huge variety of equipment specially designed for baking mini cakes in all shapes and sizes. Very little of this equipment is essential for most of the recipes in this book though you might be interested in collecting a small stash of utensils, pans, and other gadgets that will make baking easier and help achieve professional-looking results.

mini cupcake & muffin pans

These vary in sheet size and capacity and are available in metal or silicone. They're ideal for making small tartlets or for lining with mini paper muffin or cupcake bake cups.

madeleine sheets

Shell-shaped to create delicate madeleine sponge cakes, these sectioned pans are available in metal or silicone. Madeleine cake batter can be cooked in mini cupcake pans.

mini loaf pans

Ideal for small cake or bread-based recipes, these little loaves always look impressive. If you only have a few of the pans you'll need to bake the cakes in batches, or use a silicone linked loaf pan.

removable-bottomed baking pans

Some of the recipes are baked in small square, removable-bottomed pans. Regular deep removable-bottomed cake pans can be used although shallow square tart pans, about 1¼ inches deep are easier to manage.

dariole, brioche, and tartlet pans

With a base diameter of about 1¼ inches these are perfect for mini cakes. They're usually sold individually and can be expensive if buying plenty, but you can always bake in batches as they're so quick to cook. If buying tartlet pans, removable-based ones are easier to use as you can push the tartlet shells out of the pans from underneath without damaging the delicate pastry.

paper bake cups

There are so many different sizes of bake cups in a feast of striking colors. For mini cakes choose ones with a base measurement of 1¼ – 1¾ inches which is considerably smaller than a regular cupcake cup. You'll need to use a cupcake or mini muffin pan with similar-size holes as the paper alone isn't enough to support the filling.

mini silicone muffin cups

Brightly colored or pastel-shaded silicone mini muffin or cupcake cups are increasingly popular. You have a reuseable supply at hand and you don't need a sectioned pan for cooking as they sit on a regular baking sheet. (See using silicone mini muffin cups below.)

pastry bags

Reusable nylon pastry bags, available from specialty cake-decorating shops or cook shops, can be fitted with a star or plain, metal or plastic piping tip for piping, then washed and thoroughly dried before storing. They're ideal for piping large swirls of cream or frosting for decorating, or for piping neat meringues to bake. Large disposable plastic bags with the ends of the bags snipped off to accommodate the tips are useful for piping large amounts. For piping decorations such as melted chocolate a paper pastry bag is ideal.

piping tips

The recipes in this book use plain and star tips with about ½ inch diameter tip for piping meringues, cookie dough, creams, and

frostings. They're available in metal and plastic though metal ones usually give a better finish.

hand-held electric mixers

These are perfect for mixing smaller quantities of batter, cream, and icings and is a useful gadget throughout the book. Mixing can also be done by hand using a balloon whisk though it'll require a little more effort to achieve the right consistency.

cookie cutters

Several recipes require small cutters, usually round or heart shaped and between about 1¼ and 2½ inches in diameter. There are many other cutter shapes available and you can easily adapt cookie designs to make them seasonal, for example spring flowers, Christmas stockings, etc.

using silicone muffin cups

Arrange silicone cups on a baking sheet, spacing them slightly apart and fill as you would a paper bake cup. After baking allow the cakes to cool in the cups, or, if you want to remove them for serving, allow to cool for 2–5 minutes and then lift the cakes out to a wire rack to cool. The cups are dishwasher proof but may fly around during the cycle as they're so light. You'll probably find it easier to wash them by hand. After washing it's easiest to let them drain and dry thoroughly, upturned, on a dish towel so they're thoroughly dry before stacking and storing.

making & using a paper pastry bag

Cut out a 10 inch square of waxed paper. Fold it diagonally in half. Cut the paper in half, just to one side of the folded line.

Holding one piece with the long edge away from you, curl the right-hand point over to meet the center point, making a cone shape. Bring the left-hand point over the cone so the three points meet. Fold the points over several times to secure the cone. Snip off the tip and insert a piping tip, if using. Half fill the bag and fold over the ends to secure. If using the bag without a piping tip, fill the bag and fold over the open end to secure as above and then snip off the merest tip with scissors. Test how thickly the filling flows from the bag and snip off a little more from the bag if you want to pipe thicker lines.

cake-making methods

There are different processes used to make various types of cakes from sponge cakes to meringues. The following guidelines will help.

mixing sponge cakes

Most of the sponge cakes in the book are made using the "single-stage" method in which all the ingredients are simply beaten together before adding any additional ingredients like nuts, chocolate, or dried fruit. Soften the butter in the mixing bowl first (see below) and then simply beat all the ingredients together. This usually takes between 1 and 2 minutes and the consistency of the beaten ingredients will become paler in color and develop a soft, creamy consistency.

making muffins

Muffins are made by folding the wet ingredients such as eggs, milk, yogurt, and melted butter into the dry ones which you've already combined in a bowl. Once the wet ingredients are added, use a large metal

spoon and gently stir the ingredients together. Mix until they're only just combined so traces of flour are still visible. Over-beating will produce tough results.

making meringues

Use thoroughly clean dry equipment for making meringues as any grease will prevent the egg whites from peaking. Beat the egg whites until stiff so that they form firm peaks when the beater is lifted from the bowl. Add a tablespoonful of the sugar and beat for about 10 seconds before adding another tablespoonful of sugar. Repeat until all the sugar has been incorporated. The meringue should be stiff and glossy. If the sugar is added too quickly the sugar syrup will seep out during baking.

shaping scones

The easiest mistake to make when shaping scones is to roll the dough too thinly so they're flat and cookie-like. The dough once mixed should be soft but not sticky and unmanageable. Tip it onto a lightly floured surface and roll out thickly. While regular scone dough is rolled to around ¾ inch thickness, mini scones are rolled slightly thinner, i.e. about half inch as smaller shapes are cut and the baking time will be shorter.

using phyllo pastry

Phyllo pastry dries out very quickly so always keep any sheets you are not using wrapped in plastic wrap or covered with a damp cloth to stop it turning brittle and flaky. You don't need to grease pans before lining with phyllo pastry but you do need to brush each layer with butter or oil so the baked pastries are moist and sufficiently flavored.

baking & decorating techniques

Here are a few simple guidelines for queries that you might have related to baking and decorating, particularly if you're a first-time baker.

softening butter

Unless the weather is very hot or the kitchen is really warm, butter is still slightly too firm to use even if it's been out of the refrigerator a while. For sponge-based cakes and buttercream, cut the measured butter into small pieces and soften in the microwave.

Use medium power and heat in short bursts until the butter is soft enough to be pushed into with your finger. Take care not to leave it too long or it'll melt completely.

melting chocolate

There are three ways of melting chocolate to use for decorating cakes or adding to other ingredients for frostings and cake mixes.

To melt on the stovetop, chop the chocolate into small pieces and put in a heatproof bowl. Rest the bowl over a pan of very gently simmering water, making sure the base of the bowl doesn't come in contact with the water. Once the chocolate starts to melt, turn off the heat and leave until completely melted, stirring once or twice until no lumps remain. Don't |let any water get into the bowl, e.g. steam from the pan, or the chocolate will solidify and cannot be melted again.

To melt in the microwave, chop the chocolate

into small pieces and put in a heatproof bowl. Melt the chocolate in 1-minute spurts, checking frequently. Take care, particularly when melting white or milk chocolate as they have a higher fat and sugar content and are more likely to scorch.

To melt in the oven, chop the chocolate into small pieces and put in a small oven-proof dish or bowl. Put in the switched-off oven after baking and leave until melted. Sometimes chocolate is melted with other ingredients such as butter, syrup, or milk. Check more frequently as the melting time will usually be quicker.

lining pans

Sponge-based cakes and tray bakes usually require waxed or parchment paper lined pans. Brush the pan with melted butter first, then cut a length of paper which is long enough to cover the base of the pan and come up two sides. Press into position. Cut two further rectangles to line the ends of the pan. Grease the paper so the cake mixture is not prevented from rising by sticking to the paper.

filling paper or silicone cups

Cake mixtures rise as they bake so don't overfill the cases or the mixture will spill over the sides during baking. Unless a recipe states otherwise fill the cases with cake batter so they're no more than two-thirds full. If you have excess, bake a second batch. You can pile muffin mixture up a little in the center as they dome up as they bake without spilling over.

baking blind

Pastry tartlet shells are usually baked "blind" before filling so the pastry is partially cooked and crisped up before the filling is added. Once you've lined the shells with pastry, cut circles of waxed or parchment paper about 2 inches larger than the shells and push down into the shells. Fill with pie weights (available from cook shops) or with a dry ingredient such as lentils or beans that you can label and reuse for this purpose. After the pastry is baked, lift out the paper and weights. The pastry is then usually baked for a few minutes more before filling.

whipping cream

It's very easy to over-whip heavy cream for use as a filling or decoration whether used alone or flavored with other ingredients. Its flavor becomes less creamy and the texture grainy. Use a hand-held electric mixer or balloon whisk and beat the cream until it only just starts to hold its shape. Bear in mind that the cream will continue to thicken up even as you spread it or transfer it to a pastry bag.

storing cakes and mini bakes

Most mini cakes, cookies, and pastries are best served freshly baked. However if you want to make them ahead, they can be stored in an airtight container for up to 24 hours before serving. Sponge-based cakes can be frozen and thawed completely before decorating. Muffins and scones are always best served freshly baked, even still slightly

warm from the oven. Alternatively make them ahead and freeze for reheating in the oven to revive their freshly baked texture and flavor. Crisp meringues and macaroons have a longer storage life. Undecorated they will store for several days before sandwiching with fillings or whipped cream.

royal icing

Made with royal icing sugar, which is superfine, and does not clog, so is suitable for more elaborate decoration work. For 1 quantity to use in the recipes, beat 1¾ cups royal icing sugar in a bowl with enough cold water (about 5 teaspoons) to make icing with a softly peaking consistency.

cupcakes

lemon & limoncello cupcakes

Makes **16**
Preparation time **20 minutes**,
  plus cooling
Cooking time **12 minutes**

¼ cup **lightly salted butter**,
  softened
¼ cup **superfine sugar**
½ cup **self-rising flour**
finely grated zest of **1 lemon**,
  plus 1 tablespoon of the
  juice
1 **egg**
3 tablespoons **limoncello
  liqueur**

Frosting
5 tablespoons **lemon curd**
⅓ cup **unsalted butter**,
  softened
½ cup **confectioners' sugar**,
  plus extra for dusting

Place 16 mini silicone muffin cups on a baking sheet.

Put the butter, sugar, flour, lemon zest, and egg in a
bowl and beat with a hand-held electric mixer until light
and creamy. Divide the batter between the muffin cups.

Bake in a preheated oven, 350°F, for 10–12 minutes
until risen and just firm. Allow to cool in the cups for
2 minutes before transferring to a wire rack. Drizzle 2
tablespoons of the limoncello over the cakes and allow
to cool completely.

Reserve 2 tablespoons of the lemon curd and spread
the remainder over the cakes with a spatula.

Make the frosting by putting the unsalted butter,
confectioners' sugar, remaining limoncello, reserved
lemon curd, and the lemon juice in a bowl and beating
well until smooth and creamy. Place in a pastry bag
fitted with a star tip and pipe swirls on top of each cake.
Serve lightly dusted with confectioners' sugar.

For rhubarb & orange cupcakes, make the batter as
above, using the finely grated zest of ½ orange instead
of lemon. Divide between the muffin cups. Cut 4 oz
rhubarb into very thin diagonal slices and toss with 4
teaspoons superfine sugar and a good pinch of ground
ginger. Pile on top of the cake bases and sprinkle
with 2 tablespoons crushed slivered almonds. Bake as
above and serve dusted with confectioners' sugar.

very chocolatey muffins

Makes **16**
Preparation time **10 minutes**
Cooking time **15 minutes**

1 cup **self-rising flour**
¼ cup **unsweetened cocoa powder**
½ teaspoon **baking powder**
¼ cup **light brown sugar**
½ cup **chopped milk chocolate**
1 **egg**
5 tablespoons **milk**
¼ cup **lightly salted butter,** melted

Place 16 mini silicone muffin cups on a baking sheet.

Sift the flour, cocoa powder, and baking powder into a bowl. Stir in the sugar and chopped chocolate.

Beat the egg in a separate bowl and stir in the milk and melted butter. Using a large metal spoon, stir the ingredients together until only just combined. Divide between the muffin cups.

Bake in a preheated oven, 400°F, for 15 minutes until risen and just firm. Serve warm or cold.

For spiced pear muffins, sift 1 cup self-rising flour and ½ teaspoon ground pumpkin pie spice into a bowl and stir in ¼ cup rolled oats, ½ teaspoon baking powder, and ¼ cup superfine sugar. Peel, core, and dice 1 ripe pear and add to the bowl with 3 tablespoons golden raisins. Mix together the egg, milk, and butter as above and add to the bowl. Divide between the muffin cups and bake as above. Serve dusted with confectioners' sugar.

blueberry friands

Makes **16**
Preparation time **10 minutes**
Cooking time **15 minutes**

¼ cup **lightly salted butter**
2 **egg whites**
¼ cup **plain flour**
¾ cup **confectioners' sugar**,
   plus extra for dusting
⅓ cup **ground almonds**
½ teaspoon **almond extract**
½ cup **blueberries**

Place 16 mini silicone muffin cups on a baking sheet.

Melt the butter and allow to cool. Beat the egg whites in a thoroughly clean bowl until frothy but not turning white and peaking.

Sift the flour and confectioners' sugar into the bowl then add the ground almonds. Stir the almond extract into the melted butter and add to the bowl. Stir the ingredients gently together until combined. Divide between the muffin cups so each is about three-quarters full and place several blueberries on top of each.

Bake in a preheated oven, 400°F, for 12–15 minutes until risen and just firm to the touch. Leave in the cups for 5 minutes then transfer to a wire rack to cool. Serve warm or cold dusted with confectioners' sugar.

For hazelnut & apricot friands, lightly toast ⅓ cup hazelnuts and grind in a food processor. Chop ⅓ cup plump dried apricots into very small pieces. Prepare the cakes as above using the hazelnuts instead of the almonds, vanilla extract instead of the almond extract, and placing a little pile of chopped apricots on the centers instead of the blueberries

marsala raisin & coffee muffins

Makes **16**
Preparation time **15 minutes**,
  plus soaking
Cooking time **12 minutes**

¹/₃ cup **raisins**
4 tablespoons **Marsala**
1 teaspoon **instant espresso
  coffee powder**
1 cup **self-rising flour**
½ teaspoon **baking powder**
¼ cup **superfine sugar**
½ cup **plain yogurt**
1 **egg,** beaten
2 tablespoons **vegetable oil**

Icing
½ teaspoon **espresso coffee
  powder**
6 tablespoons **confectioners'
  sugar**, sifted

Put the raisins and Marsala in a small saucepan and heat until hot but not boiling. Pour into a bowl and allow to stand for 2 hours until the raisins have plumped up.

Place 16 mini silicone muffin cups on a baking sheet.

Mix the coffee powder with 2 teaspoons boiling water. Sift the flour and baking powder into a bowl. Stir in the sugar.

Mix together the yogurt, egg, oil, and coffee mixture and stir in the raisins and any unabsorbed liquid. Add to the dry ingredients. Using a large metal spoon, stir the ingredients together until only just combined. Divide among the muffin cups.

Bake in a preheated oven, 400°F, for about 12 minutes until risen and firm. Leave in the cups for 2 minutes then transfer to a wire rack to cool.

Make the icing by mixing the espresso coffee powder for the icing in a small bowl with 1½ teaspoons hot water until blended. Beat in the confectioners' sugar and drizzle over the muffins.

For mocha cream muffins, make the muffins as above, omitting the raisins and Marsala and replacing them with ¼ cup chopped white chocolate and 1 tablespoon unsweetened cocoa powder. After baking, mix together 2 teaspoons superfine sugar, ½ teaspoon ground cinnamon, and ½ teaspoon unsweetened cocoa powder and use to sprinkle generously over the muffins.

white chocolate raspberry cupcakes

Makes **16**

Preparation time **25 minutes**, plus cooling

Cooking time **12 minutes**

¼ cup **lightly salted butter**, softened

3 tablespoons **superfine sugar**

½ cup **self-rising flour**

1 **egg**

1½ oz **white chocolate**, chopped into small pieces

Topping

⅔ cup **raspberries**

⅔ cup **medium-fat cream cheese**

1 tablespoon **confectioners' sugar**

chocolate curls, to decorate

Place 16 mini silicone muffin cups on a baking sheet.

Put the butter, sugar, flour, and egg in a bowl and beat with a hand-held electric mixer until light and creamy. Stir in the chopped chocolate and divide between the muffin cups.

Bake in a preheated oven, 350°F, for 10–12 minutes, or until risen and just firm. allow to cool in the cups for 2 minutes before transferring to a wire rack to cool completely.

Make the topping by putting the raspberries in a bowl and crushing with a fork until broken up. Put the cream cheese and confectioners' sugar in a separate bowl and beat until smooth. Stir the crushed raspberries into the mixture until lightly combined but not completely blended. Spoon over the tops of the cakes and decorate with the chocolate curls.

For marshmallow cream cakes, make the cakes as above and allow to cool. Using a teaspoon, take a deep scoop out of the center of the cakes and spread a little raspberry or strawberry jelly in the bases. Lightly toast 16 marshmallows and push one into the center of each cake. Whip ⅔ cup heavy cream with 1 tablespoon sifted confectioners' sugar and put in a pastry bag fitted with a ½ inch star tip. Pipe swirls up around and over the marshmallows. Scatter with pink sugar sprinkles to decorate.

apricot cheesecake bites

Makes **16**
Preparation time **25 minutes**,
  plus cooling
Cooking time **25 minutes**

8 **graham crackers**
1 tablespoon **unsalted butter**,
  melted
½ cup **superfine sugar**
1 teaspoon **vanilla bean
  paste**
4 **apricots**, pitted and
  quartered
¾ cup **cream cheese**
⅓ cup plain **whole milk
  yogurt**
1 **egg**, beaten

Place 16 mini silicone muffin cups on a baking sheet.

Put the crackers in a plastic bag and crush with a rolling pin until finely ground. Tip into a bowl and mix with the melted butter. Divide between the muffin cups, pressing down firmly with the back of a teaspoon.

Put half the sugar in a saucepan with 6 tablespoons water and the vanilla bean paste and heat until the sugar dissolves. Add the apricots, cover, and cook gently for about 5 minutes until softened. Allow to cool.

Beat the remaining sugar with the cream cheese, yogurt, and egg until smooth. Spoon over the crumb bases.

Bake in a preheated oven, 350°F, for about 15 minutes or until lightly set. Allow to cool in the cups before transferring to a plate.

Drain the apricots from the syrup and place on the cheesecakes. Cook the syrup left in the saucepan for 3–4 minutes until thick and syrupy. Spoon over the apricots to serve.

For chocolate ginger cheesecakes, make the crumb base as above, using gingersnaps instead of graham crackers. Pack into the silicone cups. Finely chop 2 pieces of preserved stem ginger in syrup. Beat together ¾ cup cream cheese with ⅓ cup light brown sugar and 1 egg until smooth. Stir in the chopped ginger and 4 oz melted bittersweet chocolate and spoon over the crumb bases. Bake as above. allow to cool and serve dusted with unsweetened cocoa powder.

chocolate fudge cupcakes

Makes **16**
Preparation time **25 minutes**,
  plus cooling
Cooking time **12 minutes**

6 tablespoons **unsweetened
  cocoa powder**
¼ cup **lightly salted butter**,
  softened
½ cup **light brown sugar**
1 **egg**
1 cup **self-rising flour**
1¼ cups **raspberries**, to
  decorate

Frosting
6 tablespoons chopped
  bittersweet chocolate
1 tablespoon **milk**
2 tablespoons **lightly salted
  butter**
¼ cup **confectioners' sugar**,
  sifted, plus extra for dusting

Place 16 mini silicone muffin cups on a baking sheet.

Beat the cocoa powder with ⅓ cup boiling water in a bowl. Allow to cool.

Beat together the butter and brown sugar in a separate bowl until pale and creamy. Gradually beat in the egg. Stir in the flour and then the cocoa mixture. Divide between the muffin cups.

Bake in a preheated oven, 350°F, for 8–10 minutes until risen and just firm to the touch. Leave in the cups for 2 minutes then transfer to a wire rack to cool.

Make the frosting by putting the chocolate, milk, and butter in a small saucepan and heat gently until the chocolate has melted to make a smooth sauce. Remove from the heat. Sift the confectioners' sugar into the chocolate mixture and stir well. Use a spatula to spread the frosting over the cakes. allow to cool completely. Sprinkle with the raspberries and dust lightly with confectioners' sugar.

For caramel pecan sauce, lightly toast and chop ½ cup pecan nuts. Put ⅓ cup heavy cream in a small saucepan with ½ cup light brown sugar and ¼ cup unsalted butter. Heat gently until the sugar dissolves then bring to a boil and cook for about 5 minutes, stirring frequently until the syrup has turned to a pale caramel color. Don't let the mixture bubble for too long or it will start to burn. Immerse the base of the pan in cold water to prevent further cooking. Stir in the nuts and serve as an alternative topping for the fudge cakes.

mini minted cupcakes

Makes **50**
Preparation time **40 minutes,**
    plus cooling
Cooking time **14 minutes**

2 oz **extra-strong mints**
    (about 1 ¼ tubes)
½ cup **lightly salted butter,**
    softened
⅓ cup **superfine sugar**
2 **eggs**
1 cup **self-rising flour**
½ teaspoon **baking powder**

To decorate
½ cup chopped **bittersweet**
    chocolate
2 tablespoons chopped **milk**
    chocolate

Place 50 mini paper or foil bake (petit four) cups on a baking sheet.

Put the mints in a plastic bag and beat with a rolling pin to break them into coarse crumbs. Tip the mints into a bowl and add all the remaining cake ingredients. Beat with a hand-held electric mixer for about a minute until light and creamy. Divide the cake batter between the paper bake cups.

Bake in a preheated oven, 350°F, for 12 minutes, or until risen and just firm to the touch. Transfer to a wire rack to cool.

Melt the bittersweet and milk chocolate in separate bowls (see page 14). Put the melted milk chocolate in a paper pastry bag and snip off the merest tip. Spread the bittersweet chocolate over the cakes. Use the milk chocolate to drizzle lines over the dark chocolate, or pipe little dots. Leave in a cool place to set before serving.

For mini mint fudge cakes, make the cake batter as above, but substitute 2 tablespoons unsweetened cocoa powder for 2 tablespoons of the flour. Bake as above. Melt 7 oz white chocolate with 4 tablespoons milk, stirring until smooth. Stir in 1 ¼ cups sifted confectioners' sugar. Spread over the cooled cakes and dust with unsweetened cocoa powder.

amaretti plum cakes

Makes **16**
Preparation time **15 minutes**,
  plus cooling
Cooking time **10 minutes**

1½ oz **amaretti cookies**
3 tablespoons **light brown sugar**
¼ cup **lightly salted butter**,
  softened
1 **egg**
½ cup **self-rising flour**
½ teaspoon **baking powder**

Icing
½ cup **confectioners' sugar**,
  sifted
2 teaspoons **lemon juice**

To decorate
4 **plums**, pitted and chopped
8 **unblanched almonds**,
  chopped

Place 16 mini silicone muffin cups on a baking sheet.

Put the cookies in a plastic bag and crush with a rolling pin until finely ground. Tip into a bowl and add the sugar, butter, and egg, then sift in the flour and baking powder. Beat with a hand-held electric beater until smooth and creamy. Divide between the muffin cups.

Bake in a preheated oven, 350°F, for 10 minutes, or until risen and just firm. Allow to cool in the cups for 2 minutes before transferring to a wire rack to cool completely.

Make the icing by beating the confectioners' sugar with the lemon juice to make a smooth paste . Spread a little over the cakes and pile up with the plums and almonds. Drizzle a little more icing on top.

For apricot & ginger cakes, make the cake recipe as above, using crushed gingersnap cookies instead of the amaretti and adding 1 finely chopped piece of preserved stem ginger in syrup. Use small apricots instead of the plums. After baking, drizzle the cakes with some of the stem ginger syrup instead of the icing.

maple butter pecan cupcakes

Makes **16**
Preparation time **20 minutes**,
plus cooling
Cooking time **12 minutes**

¼ cup **lightly salted butter**,
softened
¼ cup **superfine sugar**
½ cup **self-rising flour**, sifted
1 egg
⅓ cup **pecan nuts**, finely
chopped
16 **pecan nuts,** to decorate

Maple butter
½ cup **lightly salted butter**,
softened
½ teaspoon **vanilla bean
paste**
4 tablespoons **confectioners'
sugar**, sifted
6 tablespoons **maple syrup**

Place 16 mini silicone muffin cups on a baking sheet.

Put the butter, sugar, flour, and egg in a bowl and beat
with a hand-held electric mixer until light and creamy.
Stir in the chopped pecans and divide between the
muffin cups.

Bake in a preheated oven, 350°F, for 10–12 minutes,
or until risen and just firm. Leave to cool in the cups
for 2 minutes before transferring to a wire rack to cool
completely.

Make the maple butter by beating together the butter,
vanilla bean paste, and confectioners' sugar until
smooth and creamy. Gradually blend in the maple syrup,
beating well until pale and fluffy. Place in a pastry bag
fitted with a small star tip and pipe swirls over the cakes.
Decorate with pecan nuts.

For white chocolate & macadamia cupcakes, make
the cake batter as above, using chopped macadamia
nuts instead of the pecans and adding 2 tablespoons
chopped white chocolate and ½ teaspoon almond
extract. Bake and cool as above. Melt 2 oz white
chocolate. Using a teaspoon, drizzle lines of chocolate
over the cooled cupcakes.

very fruity muffins

Makes **16**
Preparation time **10 minutes**
Cooking time **10 minutes**

½ cup **red currants**
½ cup **raspberries**
1 cup **self-rising flour**
1 teaspoon **baking powder**
¼ cup **superfine sugar**
½ cup **strawberry or
    raspberry yogurt**
1 **egg**, beaten
2 tablespoons **vegetable oil**
1 teaspoon **vanilla extract**
confectioners' sugar, for
    dusting (optional)

Pull the red currants from their stalks, if necessary, by running them between the tines of a fork. Mix with the raspberries and mash very lightly.

Place 16 mini silicone muffin cups on a baking sheet.

Sift the flour and baking powder into a bowl and stir in the sugar. Beat together the yogurt, egg, vegetable oil, and vanilla extract. Stir in the fruits. Add the mixture to the dry ingredients and mix gently together until only just combined. Divide between the muffin cups.

Bake in a preheated oven, 400°F, for about 10 minutes until risen and firm. Leave in the cups for 2 minutes then transfer to a wire rack to cool. Place a little sprig of red currants on each muffin and dust lightly with confectioners' sugar, if desired.

For gooseberry & elderflower muffins, top and tail ¾ cup gooseberries. Cut in half and put in a saucepan with 1 tablespoon water. Heat gently for 2–3 minutes until the berries start to soften. Remove from the heat and stir in 6 tablespoons elderflower cordial. Allow to cool. Complete the recipe as above, omitting the yogurt and vanilla extract and adding ¼ cup ground almonds and 1 teaspoon almond extract.

black forest bites

Makes **16**
Preparation time **20 minutes**,
    plus cooling
Cooking time **14 minutes**

¼ cup **lightly salted butter**,
    softened
¼ cup **light brown sugar**
½ cup **self-rising flour**
2 tablespoons **unsweetened
    cocoa powder**
1 **egg**
3 tablespoons **dried sour
    cherries**, chopped

Topping
½ cup chopped **bittersweet
    chocolate**
2 teaspoons **corn syrup**
⅔ cup **heavy or whipping
    cream**
2 tablespoons **kirsch**
16 pitted canned **black
    cherries**
2 tablespoons **cherry or red
    fruit preserves**

Place 16 mini silicone muffin cups on a baking sheet.

Put the butter, sugar, and egg in a bowl, sift in the flour
and cocoa powder, and beat with a hand-held electric
mixer until light and creamy. Stir in the sour cherries and
divide between the muffin cups.

Bake in a preheated oven, 350°F, for 10–12 minutes
until risen and just firm. Allow to cool in the cups for
2 minutes before transferring to a wire rack to cool
completely.

Make the topping by melting the chocolate (see page
14) and stirring in the syrup. Spoon over the chocolate
cakes so the icing trickles down the sides. Whip the
cream with the kirsch and spoon or pipe onto the cakes.
Pat the cherries dry on paper towels and place on top
of the cakes. If the preserves have a thick, jam-like
consistency, heat in a small saucepan with 2 teaspoons
water to soften, then cool slightly before drizzling over
the cakes.

For glossy chocolate sauce, put ½ cup light brown
sugar in a small saucepan with ½ cup water. Heat
gently, stirring until the sugar has dissolved, then bring
to a boil and boil for 1 minute. Remove from the heat
and stir in 7 oz chopped bittersweet chocolate and 2
tablespoons lightly salted butter. Allow the chocolate
to melt, stirring occasionally and returning the pan to
the heat if small pieces of chocolate remain. Serve as a
warm sauce with the cakes.

mini cappuccino cakes

Makes **12**
Preparation time **30 minutes**
Cooking time **14 minutes**

3 teaspoons **instant coffee
granules**
2 teaspoons **boiling water**
¾ cup **lightly salted butter,**
softened, plus extra for
greasing
¾ cup **light brown sugar**
1½ cups **self-rising flour**
2 tablespoons **unsweetened
cocoa powder**
½ teaspoon **baking powder**
3 **eggs**

To decorate
1¼ cups **heavy cream**
3 oz **dark or white chocolate
curls**

Grease the sections of a 12-hole deep muffin pan and
line the bases with disks of waxed paper.

Dissolve the coffee in the boiling water. Put the
remaining cake ingredients in a mixing bowl and beat
with a hand-held electric mixer until smooth. Stir in the
dissolved coffee. Divide among the sections and spread
the surfaces level.

Bake in a preheated oven, 350°F, for 12–14 minutes
until well risen and just firm. Allow to cool in the pan for
5 minutes, then transfer to a wire rack. Allow to cool
completely.

Slice each cake in half horizontally. Whip the cream
until softly peaking, then use to sandwich the cakes
together in pairs and spoon the remainder on the tops.
Sprinkle with the chocolate curls. These cakes are best
eaten on the day they are made.

For mini chocolate layer cakes, make the cakes as
above, omitting the coffee and replacing ¼ cup of the
flour with ¼ cup unsweetened cocoa powder. After
baking, split the cakes and spread each with a thin layer
of chocolate hazelnut spread and the whipped cream.
Decorate the tops as above.

white chocolate & lavender cups

Makes **16**
Preparation time **30 minutes**,
  plus chilling
Cooking time **2 minutes**

½ cup chopped **white
  chocolate**
16 small **amaretti cookies**
4 tablespoons **almond-
  flavored liqueur or orange
  juice**
3 **lavender flowers**, plus extra
  to decorate
finely **grated zest of ½
  orange**
3 tablespoons **superfine
  sugar**
1¼ cups **heavy cream**
white chocolate, to decorate

Melt the chocolate (see page 14). Place a teaspoonful into each of 16 mini silicone muffin cups and spread up the sides with the back of the teaspoon until evenly coated. Invert onto a baking sheet lined with nonstick parchment paper. Chill for at least 1 hour or until set. Carefully peel away the silicone cups and place the chocolate cups upright.

Place an amaretti cookie in each chocolate cup and drizzle with the liqueur or orange juice.

Pull the lavender flowers from the stalks and put in a pestle with the orange zest and sugar. Pound the ingredients to bruise and mingle the flavors together. Turn into a bowl with the cream and beat until the cream is only just holding its shape. Spoon into the cups and decorate with lavender flowers and white chocolate shavings.

Serve immediately or chill for up to 6 hours.

For white chocolate crunchies, melt 5 oz white chocolate with 1 tablespoon unsalted butter until smooth. Stir in 2 tablespoons chopped chocolate-coated honeycomb bar and 2 tablespoons diced shortbread cookies. Pack into the silicone cups and sprinkle with white chocolate curls. Allow to set for several hours before removing from the cups.

cranberry mincemeat cupcakes

Makes **16**

Preparation time **30 minutes**,
plus soaking and cooling

Cooking time **12 minutes**

²/₃ cup **dried cranberries**

1 small **dessert apple**, peeled,
cored, and diced

½ cup **mixed dried fruit**

2 tablespoons **light brown
sugar**

½ teaspoon **ground pumpkin
pie spice**

2 tablespoons **sherry or
ginger wine**

¼ cup lightly **salted butter**,
softened

¼ cup **superfine sugar**

½ cup **self-rising flour**, sifted

1 **egg**

Frosting

2 **egg whites**

1 cup **confectioners' sugar**,
sifted

¼ teaspoon **cream of tartar**

Put the dried cranberries, apple, mixed dried fruit, sugar, spice, and sherry or ginger wine in a food processor and blend very briefly until the ingredients are finely chopped but not puréed. (Or chop the fruits as finely as possible by hand before stirring in the other ingredients.) Stir well, cover and allow to stand for several hours or overnight.

Place 16 mini silicone muffin cups on a baking sheet. Put the butter, sugar, flour, and whole egg in a bowl and beat with a hand-held electric mixer until light and creamy. Divide between the cups. Bake in a preheated oven, 350°F, for 10–12 minutes, or until risen and just firm. Leave to cool in the cases, then transfer to a wire rack. Scoop out a little from the center of each cake. Pile the mincemeat and any juices onto the cakes.

Put the egg whites, confectioners' sugar and cream of tartar into a thoroughly clean heatproof bowl and place over a pan of gently simmering water, making sure the base does not rest in the water. Beat using a hand-held electric mixer for about 5 minutes until it thickens. Remove from the heat and beat for 4–5 minutes for soft peaks. Spoon or pipe the frosting over the cupcakes, swirling with a spatula to form soft peaks.

For amaretti & almond mincemeat, to replace the mincemeat above put ⅓ cup plump dried apricots in a food processor with 1 small pear, peeled, cored, and roughly chopped, ⅓ cup raisins, 3 tablespoons blanched almonds, 1 tablespoon light brown sugar, ½ teaspoon ground cinnamon, and 2 tablespoons amaretto liqueur. Blend until broken into small. Crumble in 1 oz amaretti cookies and blend to mix.

chocolate caramel shortbreads

Makes **16**
Preparation time **20 minutes**, plus cooling
Cooking time **17 minutes**

1 ¼ cups **all-purpose flour**
¼ lb (1 stick) chilled **lightly salted butter**, diced
½ cup **confectioners' sugar**, sifted
1 **egg yolk**
½ teaspoon **vanilla extract**
6 tablespoons chopped **bittersweet or milk chocolate**
½ cup **ready-made caramel sauce**

Place 16 mini silicone muffin cups on a baking sheet.

Put the flour in a food processor and add the butter. Blend until the mixture resembles fine bread crumbs, then lightly blend in the sugar. Add the egg yolk and vanilla extract and blend to a soft dough. Shape the dough into 16 small balls and press a piece into the center of each muffin cup.

Bake in a preheated oven, 400°F, for 12–15 minutes until just starting to brown around the edges. Leave in the cups for 10 minutes, then transfer to a wire rack to cool.

Melt the chocolate (see page 14). Spoon a little caramel sauce into the center of each shortbread and spread the melted chocolate on top.

For almond & cornmeal shortbreads, put ⅓ cup superfine sugar, ¾ cup ground almonds, and ½ cup cornmeal in a bowl. Add ⅓ cup softened unsalted butter and the finely grated zest of 1 lemon. Beat well until the ingredients have combined to form a thick paste. Pack spoonfuls of the mixture into the muffin cups, filling them to the tops. Bake as above and serve dusted with confectioners' sugar.

red velvet mini cakes

Makes **16**
Preparation time **20 minutes**, plus cooling
Cooking time **10 minutes**

1 cup **self-rising flour**
2 teaspoons **unsweetened cocoa powder**
¼ cup **superfine sugar**
1 small **raw beet**, coarsely grated
2 tablespoons **vegetable oil**
1 **egg**
3 tablespoons **buttermilk**
1 teaspoon **vinegar**

Frosting
6 tablespoons **full-fat cream cheese**
¼ cup **unsalted butter**, softened
1 teaspoon **vanilla bean paste**
1 cup **confectioners' sugar**, sifted
small edible **rose petals**, to decorate

Place 16 mini silicone muffin cups on a baking sheet.

Sift the flour and cocoa powder into a bowl. Stir in the sugar. Put the beetroot, oil, and egg in a food processor or blender and blend to make a smooth purée. Briefly blend in the buttermilk and vinegar. Add to the dry ingredients and mix together until combined. Divide between the muffin cups.

Bake in a preheated oven, 350°F, for 10 minutes or until risen and just firm. Leave to cool in the cups for 2 minutes before transferring to a wire rack to cool completely.

Make the frosting by beating together the cream cheese, butter, vanilla bean paste, and confectioners' sugar until smooth and creamy. Place in a piping bag with a small star nozzle and pipe swirls on top of the cakes. Decorate each with a rose petal.

For zucchini & lime cupcakes, finely grate ½ zucchini (about 3 oz), put in a small colander and sprinkle with 1 tablespoon salt. Allow to stand for 30 minutes, then rinse thoroughly in several changes of water to remove any traces of the salt. Make the cake recipe as above, but replacing the cocoa powder with 1 tablespoon ground almonds, the beet with the zucchini, and the vinegar with the grated zest of 1 lime. Decorate with the frosting, replacing the vanilla bean paste with 1 tablespoon lime juice.

gluten-free banoffi bites

Makes **24**
Preparation time **10 minutes**,
   plus cooling
Cooking time **12 minutes**

1 cup **brown rice flour**
1/3 cup **lightly salted butter**,
   softened
1/3 cup **superfine sugar**
2 teaspoons **gluten-free
   baking powder**
1 large **banana**, mashed
2 **eggs**
6 **toffees**, chopped
1 tablespoon **light brown
   sugar**
2 tablespoons **chewy banana
   slices** or **dried banana
   chips**

Line 2 x 12-hole mini muffin pans with paper bake cups.

Place the butter, superfine sugar, baking powder, banana, and eggs in a bowl and beat with a hand-held electric mixer until smooth. Stir in the toffees. Spoon the mixture into the paper cups and sprinkle with most of the brown sugar.

Bake in a preheated oven, 400°F, for 10−12 minutes until golden and just firm to the touch. Remove the cakes from the oven and transfer to a wire rack to cool.

Top with chewy banana slices or banana chips and sprinkle with the remaining sugar.

For walnut & brown sugar butterflies, make the muffin batter as above, replacing the toffees with 1/3 cup finely chopped walnuts. Bake as above and allow to cool. Thoroughly beat 1/2 cup softened unsalted butter in a bowl with 1/2 cup light brown sugar until smooth, pale, and creamy. Cut a round from the center top of each cake using a small sharp knife. Cut each round in half. Spoon or pipe the buttercream into the centers and position the halved rounds to resemble butterfly wings. Dust lightly with confectioners' sugar.

chili cornmeal cakes

Makes **16**
Preparation time **20 minutes**,
 plus cooling
Cooking time **10 minutes**

²/₃ cup **cornmeal**
¼ cup **superfine sugar**
½ teaspoon **baking powder**
⅓ cup **ground almonds**
2 tablespoons **olive oil**
2 **eggs**
juice of **1 lime**
1 medium **red chili**, seeded
 and finely sliced

Icing
2 **limes**
1 cup **fondant icing sugar**

Place 16 mini silicone muffin cups on a baking sheet.

Put the cornmeal, sugar, baking powder, and ground almonds in a bowl. Beat the oil with the eggs, lime juice, and half the chili. Add to the dry ingredients and stir to make a smooth paste. Divide between the muffin cups.

Bake in a preheated oven, 350°F, for about 10 minutes until pale golden around the edges. Leave in the cups to cool.

Make the icing by using a citrus zester to pare thin curls of zest from the limes. Squeeze and measure 4 teaspoons of the juice. Beat the fondant icing sugar with the lime juice to give a consistency that thinly coats the back of the spoon, adding a dash more juice if necessary. Stir the lime zest into the icing. Place a little on each cake and spread down to the edges with a spatula. Decorate each with one slice of chili.

For fiery chocolate cupcakes, beat together ¼ cup softened butter, ¼ cup light brown sugar, 1 egg , 6 tablespoons sifted self-rising flour, ¼ cup unsweetened cocoa powder and 1 chopped medium red chili until smooth and creamy. Divide between 16 mini silicone muffin cups on a baking sheet. Bake as above. Dissolve 2 tablespoons unsweetened cocoa powder in 2 tablespoons boiling water to make a paste and allow to cool. Beat ⅓ cup lightly salted softened butter with 1 cup sifted confectioners' sugar until smooth. Beat in the cocoa mixture and pipe over the cakes. Decorate the top of each with a thin slice of chili.

peanut caramel cupcakes

Makes **16**
Preparation time **20 minutes**,
    plus cooling
Cooking time **15 minutes**

¼ cup **lightly salted butter**,
    softened
¼ cup **light brown sugar**
½ cup **self-rising flour**
1 egg
⅓ cup **salted peanuts**, finely
    chopped, plus extra to
    decorate

Frosting
¼ cup **lightly salted butter**
½ cup **light brown sugar**
3 tablespoons **milk**
¾ cup **confectioners' sugar**

Place 16 mini silicone muffin cups on a baking sheet.

Put the butter, sugar, flour, and egg in a bowl and beat with a hand-held electric mixer until light and creamy. Stir in the chopped nuts. Divide between the muffin cups.

Bake in a preheated oven, 350°F, for 10–12 minutes, or until risen and just firm. Allow to cool in the cups for 2 minutes then transfer to a wire rack to cool completely.

Make the frosting by heating the butter, sugar, and milk in a saucepan until the sugar dissolves. Bring to a boil and boil for 1 minute until the mixture turns slightly syrupy. Remove from the heat and pour into a bowl. Sift the confectioners' sugar into the bowl and beat until the mixture is smooth and fudge-like.

Spread over the tops of the cakes with a palette knife and sprinkle with chopped peanuts.

For honey & pine nut cakes, toast and chop ⅔ cup pine nuts. Make the cakes as above, using half the pine nuts to replace the peanuts. Melt 2 tablespoons lightly salted butter in a small saucepan with 1½ tablespoons honey and 1 tablespoon light brown sugar. Bring to a boil and cook until syrupy. Remove from the heat and stir in 1 tablespoon lemon juice and the remaining pine nuts. Spoon over the cakes and serve warm.

chocolate tiramisu cups

Makes **16**
Preparation time **30 minutes**, plus chilling
Cooking time **2 minutes**

½ cup chopped **bittersweet chocolate**
4 oz bought or homemade **vanilla sponge cake**, broken into small pieces
3 tablespoons **strong espresso coffee**, cooled
3 tablespoons **Marsala, Kahlua** or **Tia Maria**
small piece of **bittersweet chocolate**, grated, to sprinkle

Frosting
1 cup **mascarpone cheese**
4 tablespoons **confectioners' sugar**, sifted
1 teaspoon **vanilla extract**
1 tablespoon **strong espresso coffee**, cooled
5 tablespoons **light cream**

Melt the chocolate (see page 14). Place a teaspoonful into each of 16 mini silicone muffin cups and spread up the sides with the back of the teaspoon until evenly coated. Invert onto a baking sheet lined with nonstick parchment paper. Chill for at least 1 hour or until set. Peel away the silicone cups and place the chocolate cups upright.

Divide the pieces of vanilla sponge cake between the chocolate cups. Mix the coffee with the liqueur and spoon over the cake.

Make the frosting by beating the mascarpone in a bowl with the confectioners' sugar and vanilla extract. Beat in the coffee and cream until evenly combined. Place in a piping bag fitted with a small star nozzle and pipe swirls on top of each case. Scatter with grated chocolate and either serve immediately or chill for up to 6 hours.

For mini trifle cups, make the chocolate cups as above. Split a 4 oz slice of Madeira cake in half and spread with 4 teaspoons raspberry or strawberry jelly. Cut into small dice and place in the chocolate cups. Drizzle with 4 tablespoons sherry and sprinkle with 2 tablespoons chopped slivered almonds. Spoon 1 tablespoon custard into each cup. Whip ⅔ cup heavy cream with 1 tablespoon confectioners' sugar until just peaking. Spoon or pipe over the cups and sprinkle with crushed toasted slivered almonds to decorate.

white chocolate coconut muffins

Makes **24**
Preparation time **15 minutes**
Cooking time **8 minutes**

1¼ cups **self-rising flour**
½ teaspoon **baking soda**
⅓ cup **superfine sugar**
1½ cups **sweetened tenderized shredded coconut**, plus 3 tablespoons for sprinkling
⅓ cup **white chocolate chips**
⅔ cup **vanilla yogurt**
1 **egg**
4 tablespoons **sunflower oil**
3 tablespoons **strawberry jelly**

Line 2 x 12-hole mini muffin pans with paper bake cups.

Sift the flour and baking soda into a bowl and add the sugar, coconut, and white chocolate chips.

Mix the yogurt, egg, and sunflower oil together in a measuring cup, using a fork and add to the the dry ingredients. Gently mix everything together until just combined. Divide among the muffin cups.

Bake in a preheated oven, 375°F, for 6–8 minutes until well risen and firm. Transfer to a wire rack.

Brush with the strawberry jelly while the muffins are still warm, and sprinkle with the remaining coconut.

For white chocolate strawberry muffins, chop 4 oz white chocolate and ⅔ cup dried strawberries into small pieces. Line a 12-hole muffin pan with small paper bake cups. Mix 2 cups self-rising flour and 1 teaspoon baking powder together in a bowl. Stir in ¼ cup superfine sugar and the chopped ingredients. Mix 1 egg with ¼ cup lightly salted butter, melted, and 6 tablespoons milk. Add to the bowl and stir until only just mixed, adding a dash more milk if the batter is dry. Divide between the cups and bake at 400°F for about 15 minutes until risen and pale golden. Serve dusted with confectioners' sugar.

mini simnel cakes

Makes **12**

Preparation time **30 minutes**, plus cooling and soaking

Cooking time **30 minutes**

1¼ cups **luxury mixed dried fruit**

3 tablespoons **brandy** or **orange-flavored liqueur**

½ cup **lightly salted butter**, softened

¼ cup **light brown sugar**

1 piece of **preserved stem ginger in syrup**, finely chopped, plus 2 tablespoons of the **ginger syrup**

2 **eggs**

1¼ cups **self-rising flour**

½ teaspoon **baking powder**

½ teaspoon **freshly grated nutmeg**

12 oz **white almond paste**

confectioners' sugar, for dusting

Put the dried fruit and brandy or liqueur into a bowl and allow to soak for 1 hour. Line a 12-hole muffin pan with paper bake cups. Put the butter, sugar, ginger, ginger syrup, and eggs in a bowl, sift in the flour, baking powder, and nutmeg and beat with a hand-held electric mixer for about a minute until smooth and creamy. Stir in the fruit and any liquid until evenly mixed.

Roll 4 oz of the almond paste into a log shape, about 2½ inches long, and cut into 12 slices. Divide half the cake batter between the cases and level with the back of a teaspoon. Place an almond paste slice over each. Cover with the remaining batter. Bake in a preheated oven, 350°F, for about 25 minutes until just firm to the touch. Transfer to a wire rack to cool.

Roll out the remaining almond paste thinly on a work surface lightly dusted with confectioners' sugar. Cut out 12 rounds with a 2 inch cookie cutter. Brush the cakes with the ginger syrup and cover each with a paste round. Flatten a small piece of paste into a thin ribbon and roll up to make a rose. Place on top of the cake. Repeat for the remaining cakes. Put on a baking sheet and heat under a moderate broiler, watching closely, until lightly toasted, then dust with confectioners' sugar.

For apricot & orange simnel cakes, make the cakes as above, replacing the nutmeg with the finely grated zest of 1 orange and the mixed dried fruit with ¾ cup chopped dried apricots and ½ cup golden raisins. After baking, cover with almond paste and brush with ginger syrup. Sprinkle with slivered almonds and heat very gently under a moderate broiler as above. Serve dusted with confectioners' sugar.

mini christmas cakes

Makes **16**
Preparation time **40 minutes**,
  plus cooling
Cooking time **15 minutes**

¼ cup **lightly salted butter**,
  softened
¼ cup **dark brown sugar**
1 **egg**
½ cup **self-rising flour**
½ teaspoon **ground pumpkin
  pie spice**
¼ teaspoon **baking powder**
⅓ cup **mixed dried fruit**
1½ tablespoons chopped
  Brazil nuts
2 tablespoons **brandy** or
  orange-flavored liqueur
2 tablespoons **apricot jelly**
8 oz **marzipan**
confectioners' sugar, for
  dusting
1¼ cups **royal icing sugar**,
  sifted
edible silver dragees, to
  decorate

Place 16 mini silicone muffin cups on a baking sheet.

Put the butter, sugar, and egg in a bowl, sift in the flour, spice, and baking powder and beat with a hand-held electric mixer until light and creamy. Beat in the dried fruit and nuts. Divide between the muffin cups.

Bake in a preheated oven, 350°F, for 15 minutes or until risen and just firm. Allow to cool in the cases for 2 minutes then transfer to a wire rack to cool.

Using a skewer or toothpick, pierce holes over the tops of the cakes and spoon over the brandy or orange liqueur. Store in an airtight container for up to 1 week.

Mix the apricot jelly with 1 teaspoon hot water and brush over the tops of the cakes. Thinly roll out the marzipan on a surface dusted with confectioners' sugar and cut out 1¾ inch rounds using a small cutter, rerolling the trimmings to make sufficient. Press onto the tops of the cakes.

Beat the royal icing sugar in a bowl with enough cold water to make a softly peaking consistency. Swirl a little over the cakes and decorate with dragees.

For Christmas tree cakes, make the cakes as above and cover with marzipan. Thinly roll out 4 oz green rolled fondant on a surface dusted with confectioners' sugar and cut out 16 simple Christmas tree shapes using a small cutter. Transfer to a parchment paper lined tray for 2–3 hours to firm up. Spread the cakes with royal icing as above and gently position a tree on top of each. Decorate with garlands of red decorator frosting, pushing silver dragees into the piping to secure.

biscuits &
cookies

viennese whirls

Makes **16**
Preparation time **15 minutes**,
  plus cooling
Cooking time **20 minutes**

1 cup **unsalted butter**,
  softened
¼ cup **superfine sugar**
2 cups **all-purpose flour**,
  sifted
1 teaspoon **vanilla extract**
3 tablespoons **raspberry or
  strawberry jelly**
vanilla sugar (see page 168),
  for sprinkling

Place 16 mini silicone muffin cups on a baking sheet.

Beat together the butter and sugar until very pale
and creamy. Beat in the flour and vanilla extract until
smooth. Place in a pastry bag fitted with a ½ inch star
tip. Pipe a little mixture into the base of each muffin
cup. Pipe a ring of the mixture on top to create nest
shapes.

Bake in a preheated oven, 350°F, for 15–20 minutes
until pale golden. Leave in the cups for 5 minutes, then
transfer to a wire rack. Impress holes into the centers of
the nests if they have expanded during cooking. Allow
to cool.

Place a little jelly in the center of each nest and
sprinkle vanilla sugar over the edges.

For chocolate thumbprint cookies, make the cookie
mixture as above, replacing ¼ cup of the flour with
¼ cup unsweetened cocoa powder. Spoon the mixture
into the muffin cups and push a hole into the center of
each, using your thumb. Bake as above and allow to
cool. Put 5 tablespoons chocolate hazelnut spread in
a pastry bag fitted with a small star tip and pipe a swirl
into the center of each.

florentines

Makes **48**

Preparation time **30 minutes**, plus cooling and setting

Cooking time about **30 minutes**

²/₃ cup **butter**, plus extra for greasing

¾ cup **superfine sugar**

4 tablespoons **heavy cream**

½ cup chopped **mixed candied peel**

¼ cup **candied cherries**, chopped

½ cup **slivered almonds**

⅓ cup **dried cranberries**

3 tablespoons **pine nuts**

½ cup **all-purpose flour**, sifted

5 oz **bittersweet chocolate**

5 oz **white chocolate**

Grease and line 2 large baking sheets with nonstick parchment paper. Heat the butter and sugar gently in a pan until the butter has melted. Increase the heat and bring to a boil. Immediately remove the pan from the heat, add the cream, mixed peel, cherries, almonds, cranberries, pine nuts, and flour. Stir well to combine.

Drop 12 heaping teaspoonfuls (a quarter of the mixture) onto each of the baking sheets, leaving a 2 inch gap between each for spreading. Bake in a preheated oven, 350°F, for 7 minutes. Remove the baking sheets from the oven.

Use a 3 inch cookie cutter to drag the edges of the cookies carefully into neat rounds so that they are about 2 inches across. Bake for 3–4 minutes more until golden around the edges. Remove from the oven and leave for 2 minutes. Use a spatula to transfer the cookies to parchment paper on a work surface, and allow to cool. Repeat with the remaining mixture. Melt the bittersweet and white chocolate in separate bowls (see page 14). Spoon into separate pastry bags, drizzle on top of the cookies and leave to set.

For pistachio & white chocolate florentines, steep ½ cup shelled pistachio nuts in boiling water for 1 minute. Drain thoroughly and rub between several sheets of paper towel to remove the skins. Peel away any remaining skins and chop the nuts into small pieces. Make the Florentines as above, replacing the pine nuts with the pistachio nuts and the cranberries with 3 tablespoons raisins. Melt 1 cup chopped white chocolate and roll the edges of the Florentines in the chocolate. Transfer to nonstick parchment paper to set.

chili & cardamom morsels

Makes **24**
Preparation time **15 minutes**
Cooking time **12 minutes**

10 **cardamom pods**
2 **egg whites**
2 teaspoons **cornstarch**
½ teaspoon **hot chili powder**
½ cup **superfine sugar**
¾ cup **ground almonds**

Grease and line a large baking sheet with parchment paper. Crush the cardamom pods using a mortar and pestle to release the seeds. Remove the shells and crush the seeds until fairly finely ground.

Beat the egg whites in a thoroughly clean bowl until peaking. Sift the cornstarch and chili powder into the bowl and sprinkle in the crushed cardamom. Add the sugar and ground almonds and gently fold the ingredients together to make a sticky paste.

Place in a pastry bag fitted with a ½ inch plain tip and pipe fingers, 2 inches long, onto the baking sheet, spacing them slightly apart.

Bake in a preheated oven, 350°F, for 10–12 minutes until crisp and pale golden. Transfer to a wire rack to cool.

For hazelnut and orange fingers, blend ½ cup blanched hazelnuts in a food processor or blender until ground. Make the fingers as above, omitting the spices and adding the finely grated zest of 1 small orange with the sugar and adding the hazelnuts instead of the ground almonds.

mini orange shortbreads

Makes about **80**
Preparation time **10 minutes**,
  plus cooling
Cooking time **12 minutes**

¼ lb plus 4 tablespoons
  (1½ sticks) chilled **unsalted
  butter**, diced, plus extra for
  greasing
2 cups **all-purpose flour**,
  sifted, plus extra for dusting
grated zest of 1 **orange**
½ teaspoon **ground pumpkin
  pie spice**
⅓ cup **superfine sugar**
2 teaspoons **cold water**

To serve
2 teaspoons **confectioners'
  sugar**
1 teaspoon **unsweetened
  cocoa powder**

Grease and line 2 large baking sheets with nonstick parchment paper.

Put the flour in a food processor, add the butter, and blend until the mixture resembles fine bread crumbs. Stir in the remaining ingredients with the measurement water and mix to form a dough.

Roll out on a lightly floured surface to a thickness of ⅛ inch. Using a ¾ inch plain cutter, cut out approximately 80 rounds and place on the baking sheets.

Bake in a preheated oven, 400°F, for 10–12 minutes until golden. Carefully transfer to a wire rack to cool.

Mix together the confectioners' sugar and cocoa powder and dust a little over the shortbreads before serving.

For lemon & cardamom shortbreads, crush 10 cardamom pods using a mortar and pestle to release the seeds. Remove the shells and crush the seeds a little more until ground. Make the shortbread as above, replacing the orange zest and pumpkin pie spice with the finely grated zest of 1 lemon and the ground cardamom and using lemon juice to replace the water. Serve dusted with confectioners' sugar.

vanilla & rosewater sables

Makes about **20**
Preparation time **30 minutes**,
  plus chilling
Cooking time **8 minutes**

1 cup **chilled unsalted butter**,
  diced, plus extra for greasing
2¼ cups **all-purpose flour**,
  sifted
1 cup **confectioners' sugar**,
  sifted
2 **egg yolks**
2 teaspoons **vanilla bean**
  paste

Buttercream
¼ cup **unsalted butter**,
  softened
¾ cup **confectioners' sugar**,
  sifted, plus extra for dusting
1 teaspoon **boiling water**
few drops of **pink food**
  coloring
1–2 teaspoons **rose water**

Grease 2 baking sheets. Put the flour and butter in a food processor and blend until the mixture resembles bread crumbs. Add the sugar, egg yolks, and vanilla bean paste and blend until the mixture comes together to form a smooth dough. Wrap in plastic wrap and chill for at least 1 hour.

Roll out half the dough thinly on a lightly floured surface to about ⅛ inch thick, and cut out heart shapes using a 1¾ inch heart-shaped cutter. Space slightly apart on a baking sheet. Roll out the remaining dough and shape more hearts. Put on the second baking sheet and reroll the trimmings for extras. Bake in a preheated oven, 400°F, for about 8 minutes, or until beginning to turn golden around the edges. Transfer to a wire rack to cool.

Beat together the butter and confectioners' sugar in a bowl until smooth. Add the boiling water, the pink food coloring, and enough of the rose water to give a delicate flavor, then beat until pale and creamy. Use the buttercream to sandwich the cookies together. Serve lightly dusted with confectioners' sugar.

For ginger & nougat sables, make the biscuits as above, using 2 teaspoons ground ginger instead of the vanilla bean paste, and organic powdered sugar to replace the white sugar. Cut out 1¾ inch circles instead of hearts. For the filling, put 3 oz pink or white nougat in a heatproof bowl with 1 tablespoon milk and rest over a bowl of simmering water until the nougat has melted. Remove from the heat and cool slightly. In a separate bowl, beat together 2 tablespoons softened butter and ¼ cup sifted confectioners' sugar until smooth. Stir in the nougat and use to sandwich the cookies together.

triple chocolate pretzels

Makes **40**

Preparation time **30 minutes**,
plus rising and setting

Cooking time **8 minutes**

1 tablespoon **butter**, melted

1½ cups **bread flour**

1 teaspoon **instant dried yeast**

2 teaspoons **superfine sugar**

large pinch of **salt**

6 tablespoons warm **water**

3 oz each **bittersweet, white,** and **milk chocolate**, broken into pieces

Glaze

2 tablespoons **water**

½ teaspoon **salt**

Grease 2 large baking sheets. Put the flour, yeast, sugar, and salt into a bowl. Add the melted butter and gradually mix in the measurement water until you have a smooth dough. Knead the dough for 5 minutes on a lightly floured surface until smooth and elastic.

Cut the dough into quarters, then cut each quarter into 10 smaller pieces. Shape each piece into a thin rope about 8 inches long. Bend the rope so that it forms a wide arc, then bring one of the ends round in a loop and secure halfway along. Do the same with the other end, looping it across the secured end. Transfer the pretzels to the baking sheets. Cover with lightly oiled plastic wrap and leave in a warm place for 30 minutes until well risen.

Mix the glaze water and salt in a bowl until the salt has dissolved, then brush this over the pretzels. Bake in a preheated oven, 400°F, for 6–8 minutes until golden brown. Transfer to a wire rack and allow to cool. Melt the dark, white, and milk chocolates in 3 separate heatproof bowls (see page 14). Using a spoon, drizzle random lines of dark chocolate over the pretzels. Leave to harden, then repeat with the white and then the milk chocolate. When set, transfer to an airtight container. Eat within 2 days.

For glossy chocolate dip, put ⅔ cup light brown sugar in a small saucepan with 6 tablespoons water and heat gently until the sugar dissolves. Bring to a boil and boil for 4 minutes until syrupy. Remove from the heat and add 2 tablespoons water. Return to the heat and cook, stirring until smooth. Add ¼ cup unsalted butter and 7 oz chopped bittersweet chocolate and heat gently, stirring, until the chocolate has melted. Stir in 6 tablespoons heavy cream and pour into a bowl. Serve with the pretzels.

vanilla fudge nuggets

Makes **16**
Preparation time **15 minutes**,
plus chilling
Cooking time **20 minutes**

¹/₃ cup **unsalted butter**,
softened
¹/₃ cup **superfine sugar**
1 **egg yolk**, plus 1 tablespoon
egg white
1 ¼ cups **self-rising flour**,
sifted, plus extra for dusting
8 pieces of **soft vanilla fudge**,
cut in half
confectioners' sugar, for
dusting

Place 16 mini silicone muffin cups on a baking sheet.

Put the butter and sugar in a bowl and beat until pale
and fluffy. Beat in the egg yolk and white, then add the
flour and mix to make a firm dough. Knead into a ball,
wrap in plastic wrap and chill for at least 30 minutes.

Divide the dough in half and press half the dough into
the muffin cups. Push a piece of fudge down into the
center of each cup. Divide the remaining dough into 16
pieces. Roll each piece into a ball using lightly floured
hands and flatten into a round roughly 2 inches in
diameter. Push a circle of dough into each cup, covering
the fudge, and press it down firmly around the edges.

Bake in a preheated oven, 375°F, for 15–20 minutes,
or until slightly risen. Leave in the cups for 5 minutes,
then transfer to a wire rack to cool. Serve lightly dusted
with confectioners' sugar.

For double-choc nuggets, make the dough as above,
replacing ¼ cup of the flour with ¼ cup unsweetened
cocoa powder. Assemble the cookies, replacing the
pieces of fudge with squares of bittersweet or milk
chocolate. After baking, dust lightly with unsweetened
cocoa powder.

white chocolate drops

Makes **20**
Preparation time **10 minutes**,
  plus chilling and cooling
Cooking time **20 minutes**

¼ cup **vegetable shortening**,
  softened
¼ cup **butter**
¼ cup **superfine sugar**
1 **egg yolk**
1 cup **brown rice flour**, plus
  extra for dusting
1 tablespoon **ground
  almonds**
¼ cup grated **white
  chocolate**
2 teaspoons **confectioners'
  sugar**, for dusting

Grease and line 2 baking sheets with nonstick parchment paper.

Put the fats and sugar in a bowl and beat together, then beat in the egg yolk followed by the remaining ingredients. Form the dough into a ball, wrap in plastic wrap, and chill for 1 hour.

Knead the dough on a lightly floured surface a little to soften it, then divide into 20 balls. Place the balls on the baking sheets and flatten them slightly with a fork.

Bake in a preheated oven, 350°F, for about 20 minutes until golden. Transfer to a wire rack to cool. Dust over a little confectioners' sugar before serving.

For dark chocolate drops, beat together ½ cup softened lightly salted butter, ½ cup light brown sugar, 1 egg, 1 teaspoon vanilla extract, 1 cup sifted self-rising flour, and ¼ cup unsweetened cocoa powder. Stir in ½ cup chopped bittersweet or milk chocolate. Take teaspoonfuls of the mixture and space slightly apart on 2 greased baking sheets. Bake at 400°F for 10 minutes until beginning to darken around the edges. Transfer to a wire rack to cool. Serve dusted with unsweetened cocoa powder.

pistachio biscotti

Makes about **24**
Preparation time **15 minutes**,
plus cooling
Cooking time **30 minutes**

2 tablespoons **lightly salted
butter**, softened, plus extra
for greasing
¼ cup **superfine sugar**
finely grated zest of 1 **lemon**
1 cup **self-rising flour**
½ teaspoon **baking powder**
1 **egg yolk**, plus 1 tablespoon
egg white
½ cup shelled **pistachio
nuts**, skinned and roughly
chopped (see page 70)

Grease a baking sheet.

Put the butter, sugar, and lemon zest in a bowl and beat
together, then sift in the flour and baking powder. Add
the egg yolk, egg white, and pistachios and mix to a
soft dough.

Divide the dough into 2 pieces and shape each roughly
into a sausage measuring about 6 inches long. Space
the 2 pieces well apart on the baking sheet and flatten
each to a depth of ½ inch.

Bake in a preheated oven, 325°F, for 20 minutes until
risen and turning pale golden. Remove from the oven
and allow to cool for 10 minutes, leaving the oven on.
Using a serrated knife, cut the cookies across into
½ inch thick slices. Return to the baking sheet, cut
sides face up and bake for 10 minutes more to crisp
up. Transfer to a wire rack to cool. Store in an airtight
container for up to 1 week.

For walnut oat cookies, mix together ½ cup sifted
self-rising flour, ½ cup rolled oats, ¼ cup chopped
walnuts, and ¼ teaspoon baking soda in a bowl. Put ¼
cup lightly salted butter, ¼ cup superfine sugar, and 1
tablespoon corn syrup in a small saucepan. Heat gently
until the butter has melted. Add to the oat mixture and
stir well to mix. Roll teaspoonfuls of the mixture into
small balls and space well apart on a greased baking
sheet. Bake as above for about 15 minutes until pale
golden. Transfer to a wire rack to cool.

birthday bundles

Makes **12 cookies** (4 bundles)
Preparation time **50 minutes**,
   plus chilling and setting
Cooking time **18 minutes**

¼ lb plus 6 tablespoons (1¾
   sticks) **chilled unsalted
   butter**, diced, plus extra for
   greasing
2¼ cups **all-purpose flour**,
   sifted, plus extra for dusting
½ cup **light brown sugar**
2 teaspoons **ground ginger**
2 **egg yolks**
2 teaspoons **vanilla bean
   paste**

To decorate
1¼ **cups confectioners'
   sugar**, sifted
5–6 teaspoons **lemon** or **lime
   juice**
different-colored **sugar
   sprinkles**
fine ribbon, in 2 colors, for
   wrapping bundles

Grease and line a baking sheet with nonstick parchment paper. Put the flour and butter in a food processor and blend until the mixture resembles bread crumbs. Add the sugar, ground ginger, egg yolks, and vanilla bean paste and blend to make a smooth dough. Wrap in plastic wrap and chill for at least 1 hour.

Roll out the dough on a lightly floured surface between ⅛ inch and ¼ inch in thickness and transfer to the baking sheet. Cut off the rough edges, but leave them in position to keep the dough in place. Cut out 12 x 2 inch squares from the dough. Bake in a preheated oven, 350°F, for 16–18 minutes or until the dough has risen slightly and is beginning to darken around the edges. Re-cut the marked lines and transfer the cookies to a wire rack to cool. Beat the confectioners' sugar in a bowl with enough of the lemon or lime juice to give a consistency that thickly covers the back of the spoon. Using a teaspoon, drizzle wavy lines of citrus glaze over the top of a cookie, then brush more around the sides.

Sprinkle with sugar sprinkles, tipping off the excess, then dip the sides in more sugar sprinkles. Transfer the cookie to the parchment paper. Repeat with the remaining cookies, then leave in a cool place to set for 2 hours. Stack the cookies in little bundles and tie with ribbon.

For ginger cream cookies, roll out the spiced dough as above and cut out rounds using a 2½ inch round cutter. Bake as above. Beat together ⅓ cup softened unsalted butter with 1 cup confectioners' sugar and ½ teaspoon vanilla extract until smooth and creamy. Use to sandwich the cookies together.

pink champagne cocktails

Makes **16**
Preparation time **45 minutes**,
 plus chilling
Cooking time **15 minutes**

¼ lb plus 6 tablespoons (1¾
 sticks) **chilled unsalted
 butter**, diced, plus extra for
 greasing
2¼ cups **all-purpose flour**,
 sifted, plus extra for dusting
1 cup **confectioners' sugar**,
 sifted
2 **egg yolks**
2 teaspoons **vanilla bean
 paste**
a few drops of **pink liquid** or
 paste food coloring
sugar sprinkles
pink-tinted silver dragees

Buttercream
1 cup **confectioners' sugar**,
 sifted
⅓ cup **unsalted butter**,
 softened

Put the flour and butter in a food processor and blend until the mixture resembles bread crumbs. Add the sugar, egg yolks, and vanilla bean paste and blend until the mixture comes together to form a smooth dough. Wrap in plastic wrap and chill for at least 1 hour.

Trace and cut out a cocktail glass shape from a picture, about 4 x 3¼ inches, for use as a template. Grease 2 baking sheets. Roll out the cookie dough thinly on a lightly floured surface to about ⅛ inch thick. Lay the template over the dough and cut around it. Place on the baking sheets, spaced slightly apart and reroll the trimmings to make 16 in all.

Bake in a preheated oven, 350°F, for 15 minutes, or until pale golden. Transfer to a wire rack to cool. Beat together the confectioners' sugar and butter with a few drops of pink food coloring and 1 teaspoon hot water. Put half the buttercream in a pastry bag fitted with a fine plain tip. Spread a little across the center of the cookies so they look like half-filled glasses. Pipe an outline of buttercream around the edges. Sprinkle the glass cavity area with sugar sprinkles. Pipe dots of buttercream for bubbles and sprinkle with the dragees.

For pumpkin-face cookies, make the dough as above, using light brown sugar instead of superfine and adding 1 teaspoon ground pumpkin pie spice and ½ teaspoon ground ginger. Roll out and cut out pumpkin shapes. Cut out triangles for eyes and nose and a small mouth from each. Bake as above. Beat enough water into 1 cup sifted royal icing sugar to make a smooth icing that coats the back of a spoon. Add a few drops of orange food coloring. Pipe outlines around the cookie edges.

shooting stars

Makes **24**

Preparation time **1 hour**, plus
  chilling, cooling and setting

Cooking time **15 minutes**

¼ lb plus 6 tablespoons (1¾
  sticks) **chilled unsalted
  butter**, diced, plus extra for
  greasing
2¼ cups **all-purpose flour**,
  sifted, plus extra for dusting
½ cup **light brown sugar**
2 teaspoons **ground ginger**
2 **egg yolks**
2 teaspoons **vanilla bean
  paste**

To decorate
1¾ cups **royal icing sugar**
a few drops each of **orange**
  and **yellow liquid** or **paste
  food colorings**
edible gold food coloring

Grease 2 baking sheets. Put the flour and butter in a
food processor and blend until the mixture resembles
bread crumbs. Add the sugar, ground ginger, egg yolks,
and vanilla bean paste and blend to make a smooth
dough. Wrap in plastic wrap and chill for at least 1 hour.

Roll out the dough on a lightly floured surface to about
⅛ inch thick and cut out shooting star-shaped cookies
using a cookie cutter. Place on the baking sheets,
spacing them slightly apart, and reroll the trimmings to
make 24 in total. Bake in a preheated oven, 350°F, for
15 minutes or until the dough has risen slightly and is
beginning to darken around the edges. Transfer to a
wire rack to cool.

Put the royal icing sugar in a bowl and beat in enough
cold water, about 5 teaspoons, to make a thick but
smooth paste. Divide the royal icing between 2 bowls
and color 1 orange and 1 yellow. Place in 2 separate
pastry bags fitted with fine tips (or use paper pastry
bags and snip off the tip). Pipe star-shaped outlines and
broken lines of piping on the tails of the stars. Leave in
a cool place to set for about 30 minutes. Use the gold
food coloring to paint highlights on the cookies.

For festive tree cookies, roll out the spiced dough as
above and cut out Christmas tree shapes using a small
cutter. Space slightly apart on the baking sheets. Lightly
toast ⅓ cup pine nuts and arrange in rows over the
cookies, pressing them in gently. Bake as above. Put
1¾ cups royal icing sugar in a bowl and beat in enough
water to make a smooth icing that thickly coats the
back of the spoon. Drizzle lines of icing over the
cookies with a teaspoon.

shoes and purses

Makes about **20**
Preparation time **1¼ hours**,
  plus cooling and setting
Cooking time **15 minutes**

1 quantity **vanilla cookie
  dough,** chilled (see page
  230)

To decorate
1 quantity **royal icing** (see
  page 15)
few drops of **pink** or **lilac
  liquid** or **paste food
  coloring**
selection of **tiny pink candies**
  or **cake decorations**

Grease 2 baking sheets. Cut out simple pictures of
a shoe and a bag from a magazine about 4 x 3¼
inches. Roll out the cookie dough on a lightly floured
surface to about ⅛ inch thick. Lay the templates over
the dough and cut around them. Place on the baking
sheets, spaced slightly apart. Reroll the trimmings to
make extras. Bake in a preheated oven, 350°F, for 15
minutes, or until pale golden. Transfer to a wire rack to
cool. Put the royal icing sugar in a bowl and gradually
beat in enough cold water, about 2 tablespoons, to make
a smooth icing that almost holds its shape. Put a little of
the icing in a pastry bag fitted with a fine plain tip. Pipe
an outline around each cookie, then add additional lines
of piping for heels, soles, and tops of boots.

Divide the remaining icing between 2 bowls. Add the
food coloring to 1 bowl. Stir a few drops of water into
each bowl until the icing forms a flat surface when left
to stand for 15 seconds. Drizzle a little of the colored
icing onto a cookie with a small teaspoon. Push the
icing into the corners. Repeat on the remaining cookies
so that some are covered in colored icing; others in
white. Before the icing dries, gently press the candies
or decorations into them. Leave to set for about 1 hour.
Pipe additional decorations on the cookies, such as
flowers and borders on the purses and tops of shoes.

For pink heart cookies, make the cookie dough as
above and cut out heart shapes. Bake as above. Beat
a few drops of pink food coloring into some royal icing.
Pipe outlines around the edges of the cookies. Add a
few drops of water to the remaining icing and use to fill
the centers of the biscuits as above.

baby shower cookies

Makes **20**

Preparation time **1 hour**, plus
cooling and setting

Cooking time **15 minutes**

¼ lb plus 6 tablespoons (1¾
sticks) **chilled unsalted
butter**, diced, plus extra for
greasing

2¼ cups **all-purpose flour**,
sifted, plus extra for dusting

1 cup **confectioners' sugar**,
sifted

2 **egg yolks**

2 teaspoons **vanilla bean
paste**

To decorate

2 cups **royal icing sugar**,
sifted

5 **pink jellybeans**, halved
lengthwise

3 oz **pale blue, pink, or yellow
rolled fondant**

10 small **blue, pink,** or **yellow
ribbon bows**

Put the butter and flour in a food processor and blend
until the mixture resembles bread crumbs. Add the
sugar, egg yolks, and vanilla bean paste and blend until
the mixture comes together to form a smooth dough.
Wrap in plastic wrap and chill for at least 1 hour.

Copy the bootie and bottle shapes opposite to make
simple templates. Grease 2 baking sheets. Roll out the
cookie dough thinly on a lightly floured surface to ⅛
inch thick. Lay the templates over the dough and, using
a small, sharp knife or craft knife, cut around them.
Place on the baking sheets, spacing them slightly apart,
and reroll the trimmings to make 20 in all. Bake in a
preheated oven, 350°F, for 15 minutes, or until pale
golden. Transfer to a wire rack to cool.

Pipe a line of icing around the edges of the cookies.
Pipe a line of circles across the ankles of the booties
and a diagonal line of piping across the center of
the bottles. Using a small teaspoon, drizzle a little of
the thinned icing onto the lower part of the bottles,
spreading it to the edges with the back of a teaspoon
and easing it into the corners with a toothpick. Spread
the icing onto the bootie-shaped cookies in the same
way, easing it around the piping across the ankles.
Secure a jellybean half, cut side down, to the top of
each bottle with a little icing. Shape a little band of
rolled fondant and secure around the bottle necks.

Leave the cookies in a cool place to set for about 30
minutes or until the royal icing is dry to the touch, then
pipe wavy lines onto the booties and over the rolled
fondant on the bottles. Secure the ribbon bows to the
booties with a dot of icing. Leave to set for 30 minutes.

scrabble cookies

Makes **30**

Preparation time **35 minutes**

Cooking time **5 minutes**, plus chilling and cooling

⅓ cup **unsalted butter**, softened, plus extra for greasing

⅓ cup **superfine sugar**

1 **egg**

½ teaspoon **vanilla extract**

2 cups **all-purpose flour**, sifted, plus extra for dusting

To decorate

12 oz **rolled fondant**

confectioners' sugar, for dusting

2–3 tablespoons **apricot jelly**

1 small tube of **colored decorator frosting**

Grease and line 2 baking sheets with nonstick parchment paper. Beat together the butter and sugar in a bowl until pale and fluffy. Gradually add the egg and vanilla extract and beat well, adding a little flour to prevent the mixture curdling. Add the flour and fold in to make a stiff dough. Wrap in plastic wrap and refrigerate for 20 minutes.

Roll out the dough on a lightly floured surface to ⅛ inch thick. Using a 1½–2 inch cookie cutter, cut out about 30 rounds, rerolling the trimmings as necessary and place on the baking sheets. Bake in a preheated oven, 350°F, for 5 minutes, or until a very pale golden color. Transfer to a wire rack to cool.

Roll out the white icing on a sugar-dusted surface to ⅛ inch thick. Cut out 30 rounds, using a 1½–2 inch cutter. Using a clean paintbrush, paint a little of the jelly on each cookie to ensure that the icing will stick, place the icing shapes on the cookies and press down lightly. Using the colored decorator frosting, write a letter on each cookie to spell out the name or message.

For homemade rolled fondant icing, put 1 tablespoon egg white in a bowl with 1 tablespoon liquid glucose and 1 cup sifted confectioners' sugar and beat to a smooth paste. Gradually work in an additional 1¼ cups confectioners' sugar, stirring well until the mixture is very firm. Turn out onto the work surface and knead to a smooth paste, which should be firm and rollable, not sticky. Work in a little more confectioners' sugar if necessary. Wrap tightly in several thicknesses of plastic wrap and store until ready to use.

slices &
traybakes

chocolate blondie bites

Makes about **36**
Preparation time **15 minutes**
Cooking time **27 minutes**

3 tablespoons **lightly salted butter**, plus extra for greasing
8 oz **white chocolate**
2 **eggs**
¼ cup **superfine sugar**
1 teaspoon **vanilla bean paste**
¾ cup **self-rising flour**, sifted
⅓ cup **blanched almonds**, roughly chopped
confectioners' sugar, for dusting

Grease and line a 7 inch square cake pan with nonstick parchment paper.

Chop half the chocolate into small pieces and set aside. Roughly chop the remainder and put in a heatproof bowl with the butter. Rest the bowl over a saucepan of gently simmering water and leave until melted.

Beat together the eggs, sugar, and vanilla bean paste in a separate bowl. Beat in the melted chocolate mixture. Add the flour, almonds, and chopped chocolate and stir well. Turn into the pan and spread into the corners.

Bake in a preheated oven, 375°F, for about 25 minutes, or until the surface is golden and the center feels just firm to the touch. allow to cool completely before removing from the pan. Dust with confectioners' sugar and cut into small squares.

For gluten-free chocolate brownies, grease and line an 11 x 8 inch shallow baking pan with nonstick parchment paper. Chop 8 oz milk chocolate into small pieces. Melt 8 oz bittersweet chocolate with 1 cup unsalted butter, stirring frequently until smooth. In a separate bowl, beat together 3 eggs and ¾ cup light brown sugar until turning foamy. Beat in the chocolate mixture. Sift ¾ cup gluten- and wheat-free all-purpose white flour and 2 teaspoons gluten-free baking powder into the bowl. Add the chopped chocolate and ¾ cup walnut pieces. Turn into the pan, level the surface, and bake as above, adding a little extra cooking time if the surface feels very soft.

cherry bakewells

Makes about **30**
Preparation time **20 minutes**,
  plus chilling and cooling
Cooking time **1 hour**

11½ oz **prepared dessert shortcrust pastry**
6 tablespoons **cherry preserves**
½ cup **lightly salted butter**, softened
½ cup **superfine sugar**
2 **eggs**
1 teaspoon **almond extract**
1 cup **ground almonds**
1 cup **self-rising flour**
½ teaspoon **baking powder**
1 cup **candied cherries**, halved
⅓ cup **slivered almonds**

Glaze
½ cup **confectioners' sugar**, sifted
2 teaspoons **lemon juice**

Roll out the pastry thinly on a lightly floured surface and use to line the base and sides of an 11 x 7 inch shallow baking pan. Chill for 30 minutes.

Line the pie shell with nonstick parchment paper and pie weights. Bake in a preheated oven, 400°F, for 15 minutes. Remove the paper and weights and cook for 5 minutes more. Reduce the oven temperature to 350°F.

Spread the cherry preserves over the base of the pie shell. Put the butter, sugar, eggs, almond extract, and ground almonds in a bowl, sift in the flour and baking powder, and beat with a hand-held electric mixer until smooth and creamy. Stir in the cherries.

Spoon the filling out into the pie shell, spreading it gently so you don't dislodge the preserves. Level with the back of a spoon and sprinkle with the slivered almonds. Bake for about 40 minutes until risen and just firm to the touch. Allow to cool in the pan.

Make the glaze by beating together the confectioners' sugar and lemon juice. Remove the cake from the pan and drizzle with the glaze. Serve cut into small squares.

For homemade cherry preserves, put 2 cups halved and pitted cherries in a large saucepan with the juice of 2 lemons and 2 tablespoons water. Cook gently for about 5 minutes until the cherries have softened. Add 2 cups granulated sugar and heat gently until the sugar has dissolved. Cook very gently, stirring occasionally, for about 40 minutes until the liquid has reduced and thickened. Transfer to clip-top preserving jars or jam jars and cover with lids. Allow to cool, then refrigerate for up to 3 months.

tropical ginger cake

Makes **20 squares**
Preparation time **30 minutes,**
  plus cooling
Cooking time **25 minutes**

²/₃ cup **butter**, plus extra for
  greasing
½ cup **light brown sugar**
3 tablespoons **corn syrup**
2 cups **self-rising flour**
1 teaspoon **baking powder**
3 teaspoons **ground ginger**
¾ cup **shredded coconut**
3 **eggs**, beaten
7 oz can **pineapple rings**,
  drained and chopped

Lime frosting
½ cup **unsalted butter**,
  softened
1¾ cups **confectioners'**
  sugar, sifted
grated zest and juice of **1 lime**

To decorate
ready-to-eat dried papaya
  and **apricot**, diced
few **dried coconut shavings**,
  for sprinkling

Grease and line the base of a 7 x 11 inch roasting pan with nonstick parchment paper.

Heat the butter, sugar, and syrup gently in a saucepan, stirring until melted.

Mix the dry ingredients together in a mixing bowl, then stir in the melted butter mixture and beat together until smooth. Stir in the eggs, then the chopped pineapple, Pour the mixture into the pan, and spread the surface to make level.

Bake in a preheated oven, 350°F, for about 20 minutes until well risen and the cake is firm to the touch. Allow to cool in the pan for 10 minutes then loosen the edges then transfer to a wire rack.

Make the lime frosting by beating the butter, confectioners' sugar, and half the lime zest and juice together to make a smooth fluffy mixture. Turn the cake over so the top is uppermost, then spread with the lime frosting. Decorate with a sprinkling of the remaining lime zest, the ready-to-eat dried fruits, and coconut shavings. Cut into 20 pieces to serve.

For ginger muffin slice, grease and line a 1½–2 lb loaf pan with nonstick parchment paper. Beat together ½ cup lightly salted butter, melted, ¾ cup milk, and 1 egg. Mix together 2 cups all-purpose flour, 2 teaspoons baking powder, 2 teaspoons ground ginger, ²/₃ cup superfine sugar, ¼ cup rolled oats, and ½ cup raisins in a bowl. Stir in the milk mixture until just combined and turn into the pan. Bake in a preheated oven, 350°F, for about 45 minutes until risen and just firm. Dust with superfine sugar and serve freshly baked.

sticky toffee & date slice

Makes **24 squares**
Preparation time **25 minutes**,
  plus cooling
Cooking time **55 minutes**

1 cup **lightly salted butter**,
  softened, plus extra for
  greasing
1 ¼ cups chopped **pitted**
  dates
²/₃ cup **water**
²/₃ cup **heavy cream**
¾ cup **light brown sugar**
½ cup **superfine sugar**
2 teaspoons **vanilla bean**
  paste
3 **eggs**
1 ½ cups **self-rising flour**
½ teaspoon **baking powder**

Grease and line an 11 x 7 inch shallow baking pan with nonstick parchment paper. Put half the dates in a saucepan with the measurement water and bring to a boil. Reduce the heat and cook very gently for 5 minutes or until the dates are pulpy. Turn into a bowl and allow to cool. Put the cream, brown sugar, and 6 tablespoons of the butter in a small saucepan and heat gently until the sugar dissolves. Bring to a boil and boil for about 5 minutes until thickened and caramelized. Allow to cool.

Put the remaining butter in a bowl with the superfine sugar, vanilla bean paste, and eggs, sift in the flour and baking powder and beat with a hand-held electric mixer until pale and creamy. Beat in the cooked dates and 6 tablespoons of the caramel mixture. Turn into the pan and level the surface. Sprinkle with the remaining dates.

Bake in a preheated oven, 350°F, for 25 minutes, or until just firm. Spoon the remaining caramel over the top and return to the oven for about 15 minutes until the caramel has firmed up. Transfer to a wire rack to cool.

For cider-glazed apple slice, grease the pan as above. Put ¾ cup lightly salted softened butter, ¾ cup superfine sugar, 1¾ cups sifted self-rising flour, ½ teaspoon baking powder, 1 teaspoon ground pumpkin pie spice, and 3 eggs in a bowl and beat with a hand-held electric mixer until smooth and creamy. Stir in ⅓ cup golden raisins and spread in the pan. Core and slice 2 small red apples and sprinkle over the surface. Bake as above for about 40 minutes or until just firm. Put 6 tablespoons hard cider in a saucepan and heat until reduced to about 1 tablespoon. Cool and mix with ¾ cup sifted confectioners' sugar until smooth. Drizzle over the cake.

coconut & rose water slice

Makes **25 squares**
Preparation time **20 minutes**,
  plus cooling
Cooking time **40 minutes**

4 oz **almond** or **coconut
  cookies**
3 tablespoons **unsalted
  butter**, melted
1¾ cups **coconut milk**
²/₃ cup **heavy cream**
2 **eggs** plus 4 **egg yolks**
¹/₃ cup **superfine sugar**
2 tablespoons **all-purpose
  flour**
1 teaspoon **rose water**
2 oz **rose Turkish delight**,
  chopped
pink food coloring (optional)

Dampen a 7 inch square, removable-bottomed shallow cake pan and line with a square of plastic wrap that comes up and over the sides. Put the cookies in a plastic bag and crush with a rolling pin. Mix with the melted butter and tip into the pan. Pack down well. Pour the coconut milk and cream into a saucepan and heat until bubbling around the edges. Put the eggs, egg yolks, sugar, flour, and rose water in a bowl and beat until smooth. Pour the warmed milk over the egg mixture, beating well. Strain through a sieve into a measuring cup and spoon carefully over the cookie base so you don't dislodge too many crumbs.

Place a roasting pan of hot water on the lower oven shelf and place the cake pan on the upper shelf. Bake at 325°F for 35 minutes until the surface feels set but is still slightly wobbly. Leave to cool in the pan.

Put the Turkish delight in a small saucepan with 2 tablespoons water and heat very gently until melted, stirring frequently. Add a drop of pink food coloring, remove the slice from the pan, and use a teaspoon to drizzle lines of syrup across the surface. Cut into squares.

For coconut-frosted pineapple slice, beat ³/₄ cup softened unsalted butter, ³/₄ cup light brown sugar, 3 eggs, 1³/₄ cups sifted self-rising flour, and 1 teaspoon ground cinnamon together in a bowl and spread into a greased and lined 11 x 7 inch shallow baking pan. Sprinkle with ³/₄ cup chopped candied pineapple and bake at 350°F for about 40 minutes, or until just firm. Heat 5 tablespoons light cream and 2 oz creamed coconut in a small pan until the coconut has melted. Turn into a bowl and beat in 1 tablespoon lime juice and 2½ cups sifted confectioners' sugar until smooth. Spread over the top of the slice.

buttery breton cake

Makes **25 squares**
Preparation time **25 minutes**,
  plus chilling and cooling
Cooking time **45 minutes**

225 g (7½ oz) **self-rising
  flour**, plus extra for dusting
1½ cups **confectioners'
  sugar**
2 tablespoons **vanilla sugar**
  (see page 168) plus extra for
  dusting
¼ lb plus 6 tablespoons (1¾
  sticks) chilled **lightly salted
  butter**, diced, plus extra for
  greasing
5 **egg yolks**, plus 1 beaten
  egg, to glaze
½ cup **strawberry jam**

Sift the flour and confectioners' sugar into a food processor, add the vanilla sugar and butter and blend until the mixture resembles coarse bread crumbs. Add the egg yolks and blend to make a thick paste. Wrap in plastic wrap and chill for at least 3 hours or overnight.

Grease and line a 7–7½ inch square shallow baking pan with nonstick parchment paper. Press half the dough into the pan, spreading it into the corners with your fingers so the dough forms an even layer. Spread the jam over the dough, leaving ½ inch clear around the edges. Roll out the remaining dough on a floured surface to the same dimensions as the pan and lift into place. Press down gently and brush with beaten egg.

Bake in a preheated oven, 375°F, for 40–45 minutes until risen and deep golden. Allow to cool in the pan before transferring onto a flat plate or board. Dust lightly with vanilla sugar and cut into 25 squares.

For homemade strawberry jam, tip 6 cups strawberries into a large saucepan or preserving pan and add the juice of 4 lemons. Cook gently for about 10 minutes until the strawberries are soft and mushy. Add 4 cups granulated or preserving sugar and heat until the sugar dissolves. Bring to a boil and boil for about 15–20 minutes until setting point is reached. To test for setting point, put a teaspoonful of the jam on a chilled saucer and place in the refrigerator for 2 minutes. Push the cooled jam with your finger. If the surface wrinkles, then setting point is reached. If still syrupy, boil the jam for a little longer. Avoid boiling the jam for too long or it will lose its strawberry flavor. Pot into sterilized jars, then cover and label.

passion cake squares

Makes **16**

Preparation time **10 minutes**, plus cooling

Cooking time **1 hour**

butter, for greasing

1 cup **brown rice flour** , plus extra for dusting

2 teaspoons **baking powder**

1 teaspoon **xanthan gum**

1 teaspoon **ground cinnamon**

1 ½ cups **superfine sugar**

²/₃ cup **canola** or **corn oil**

2 **eggs**, beaten

few drops of **vanilla extract**

2 cups **grated carrots**

¾ cup **shredded coconut**

6 tablespoons **canned crushed pineapple**, drained

⅓ cup **golden raisins**

Topping

¾ cup **cream cheese**

2 tablespoons **honey**

½ cup chopped **walnuts** (optional)

Grease an 8 inch square cake pan and dust with flour.

Sift together the flour, baking powder, xanthan gum, and cinnamon in a large bowl. Add the sugar, oil, eggs, and vanilla extract and beat well. Fold in the carrots, coconut, pineapple, and golden raisins. Turn into the tin and level the surface.

Bake in a preheated oven, 350°F, for about 1 hour, or until a skewer inserted in the centre comes out clean. Allow to cool in the pan.

Beat together the cream cheese and honey and spread over the cake, then sprinkle the nuts on top, if using. Cut into 16 squares.

For mango & ginger cakes, prepare the cake batter as above, using 2 teaspoons ground ginger instead of the cinnamon. Peel and pit 1 small ripe mango and chop into small pieces. Fold into the batter with the carrots, coconut, and ⅓ cup chopped Brazil nuts, omitting the pineapple and golden raisins. Bake as above. Finely chop ⅓ cup candied ginger. Mix ½ cup confectioners' sugar with 1 ½–2 teaspoons water to make a glaze. Drizzle over the cake and sprinkle with the ginger.

stollen slice

Makes **15 slices**
Preparation time **30 minutes**,
plus rising
Cooking time **25 minutes**

3 tablespoons **salted butter**,
plus extra for greasing
1 cup **bread flour**, plus extra
for dusting
1 ½ teaspoons **instant dried
yeast**
½ teaspoon **ground pumpkin
pie spice**
2 tablespoons **superfine
sugar**
6 tablespoons **warm milk**
½ cup **golden raisins**
3 tablespoons chopped
almonds
2 tablespoons chopped
candied peel
5 oz **marzipan**
confectioners' sugar, for
dusting

Grease a large loaf pan with a base measurement
of about 10 x 4 inches. Put the flour, yeast, pumpkin
pie spice, and sugar in a bowl. Melt 2 tablespoons of
the butter, mix with the milk, and add to the bowl. Mix
with a round-bladed knife to make a soft but not sticky
dough. Turn out onto a lightly floured surface and knead
for 10 minutes until smooth and elastic. (Alternatively
use a stand mixer with a dough hook and knead for 5
minutes.) Place in a lightly oiled bowl, cover with plastic
wrap, and allow to rise in a warm place for about 1 ½
hours or until doubled in size.

Turn the dough out onto a floured surface and knead
in the golden raisins, almonds, and candied peel.
Cover loosely with a dish towel and allow to rest for
10 minutes. Roll out the dough on a floured surface to
a 10 x 8 inch rectangle. Roll the marzipan under the
palms of your hands to form a log shape about 9 inches
long and flatten to about ¼ inch thick. Lay the marzipan
down the length of the dough, slightly to one side, and
fold the rest of the dough over it. Transfer to the pan
and press down gently.

Cover loosely with oiled plastic wrap and allow to rise
in a warm place for about 30 minutes until slightly risen.
Remove the plastic wrap. Bake in a preheated oven,
425°F, for 25 minutes until risen and golden. Leave for
5 minutes, then turn out of the pan, place on a wire rack,
cover with a sheet of foil, and place a couple of food
cans, or package of sugar, on top to keep the stollen
compact while cooling, and cool on a wire rack. Melt
the remaining butter and brush over the bread. Dust
generously with confectioners' sugar.

lemon drizzle bites

Makes **25**
Preparation time **15 minutes**
Cooking time **25 minutes**

½ cup **lightly salted butter**,
   softened, plus extra for
   greasing
½ cup **superfine sugar**
finely grated zest and juice of
   2 large **lemons**
2 **eggs**, beaten
1 cup **self-rising flour**, sifted
⅔ cup **ground almonds**
⅓ cup **granulated sugar**

Grease and line an 8 inch square, or similar-size, removable-bottomed pan with nonstick parchment paper. Grease the paper.

Beat together the butter, superfine sugar, and lemon zest until light and fluffy. Gradually beat in the eggs, a little at a time, adding a little flour to prevent the mixture curdling. Add the remaining flour and ground almonds and fold the ingredients together gently until just combined. Turn into the pan and level the surface.

Bake in a preheated oven, 350°F, for about 25 minutes until just firm to the touch. Transfer to a wire rack to cool. While still warm, sprinkle the granulated sugar in a thick layer over the cake and drizzle with the lemon juice. Allow to cool completely and cut into 25 small slices to serve.

For almond-coffee cake, sprinkle 2 teaspoons espresso coffee powder into 2 tablespoons boiling water. Make the cake batter as above, omitting the lemon zest, and turn into the pan. Spoon the coffee mixture over the batter so it is fairly evenly distributed. Use a knife to swirl the coffee mixture into the batter to produce a rippled appearance. Toss ½ cup slivered almonds with 1 tablespoon superfine sugar and ½ teaspoon ground pumpkin pie spice, and sprinkle over the surface. Bake as above.

pomegranate & ginger slice

Makes about **20 squares**
Preparation time **25 minutes**,
plus cooling
Cooking time **50 minutes**

1/3 cup **unsalted butter**, plus
extra for greasing
1¾ cups **all-purpose flour**
1 teaspoon **baking soda**
6 tablespoons **milk**
1 **egg**
½ cup **dark brown sugar**
1/3 cup **molasses**
3 pieces of **preserved stem
ginger in syrup**, chopped

Topping
1¼ cups **pomegranate juice**
2 tablespoons **honey**
1 **pomegranate**

Grease and line 2 loaf pans, each with a base measurement of approximately 8 x 3¼ inches, with nonstick parchment paper.

Sift the flour and baking soda into a bowl. Beat together the milk and egg. Put the sugar, molasses, and butter in a saucepan and heat gently until the butter melts and the sugar dissolves. Remove from the heat and add to the milk mixture along with the chopped ginger. Add to the dry ingredients and stir well until combined using a large metal spoon. Turn into the pans and level the surface.

Bake in a preheated oven, 325°F, for 30 minutes, or until just firm to the touch and a skewer inserted in the center comes out clean. Allow to cool in the pans, then turn out onto a wire rack.

Pour the pomegranate juice into a saucepan and bring to a boil, then boil for about 15 minutes until thick and syrupy and reduced to about 3 tablespoons. Stir in the honey. Halve the pomegranate and push the halves inside out to release the fleshy seeds, discarding any white membrane, and sprinkle over the cakes. Drizzle with the syrup and cut into small squares to serve.

For golden raisin & lemon gingerbread, make the gingerbread mixture as above, reducing the milk by 2 tablespoons and sprinkling ½ cup golden raisins over the mixture in the pan. After baking, allow to cool, then drizzle with lines of glacé icing made by mixing together ¾ cup sifted confectioners' sugar with 2 teaspoons lemon juice.

cookies & cream fudge

Makes **36 pieces**
Preparation time **10 minutes**,
plus cooling and chilling
Cooking time **15 minutes**

½ cup **butter**, plus extra for
greasing
¾ cup **evaporated milk**
2 cups **superfine sugar**
3 tablespoons **water**
2 teaspoons **vanilla extract**
6 tablespoons chopped
bittersweet chocolate
8 **Oreo** or **bourbon cookies**,
chopped

Grease a 4 cup loaf pan.

Heat the butter, evaporated milk, superfine sugar, measurement water, and vanilla extract gently together in a heavy saucepan, stirring until the sugar has dissolved. Bring to a boil and boil the mixture for 10 minutes, stirring all the time. Test to see if it is ready by carefully dropping ½ teaspoon of the mixture into some cold water—it should form a soft ball. Pour half the fudge mixture quickly into a heatproof pitcher. Add the chocolate to the remaining fudge mixture in the pan and stir to melt.

Pour half the chocolate fudge into the base of the loaf pan, then carefully sprinkle with half the cookies. Pour the vanilla fudge on top and sprinkle with the remainder of the cookies. Finish with a final layer of chocolate fudge. Cool, cover with plastic wrap, and chill overnight.

Turn out the fudge onto a board and cut into pieces.

For chocolate, orange, & walnut fudge, prepare the fudge mixture as above, stirring in 6 tablespoons chopped orange-flavored dark chocolate in place of the bittersweet chocolate. Replace the cookies with ⅔ cup chopped walnuts. Finish as above.

sour cherry buns

Makes **16**
Preparation time **30 minutes**,
  plus rising
Cooking time **25 minutes**

1 ½ cups **bread flour**, plus
  extra for dusting
2 teaspoons **instant dried
  yeast**
3 tablespoons **superfine
  sugar**
finely grated zest of 1 **lemon**,
  plus 2 **teaspoons juice**
¼ cup **salted butter**, softened,
  plus extra for greasing
1 **egg**
6 tablespoons **warm milk**
½ teaspoon **almond extract**
²/₃ cup **dried sour cherries**,
  chopped
2 tablespoons **light brown
  sugar**
2 tablespoons **corn syrup**

Put the flour, yeast, sugar, and lemon zest in a bowl. Melt 3 tablespoons of the. Beat the egg with the milk, melted butter, and almond extract and add to the bowl. Mix with a round-bladed knife to make a soft but not sticky dough. Turn out onto a lightly floured surface and knead for 10 minutes until smooth and elastic. Place in a lightly oiled bowl, cover with plastic wrap, and allow to rise in a warm place for 1 ½ hours or until doubled in size.

Grease a 7 inch square cake pan, preferably removable bottomed. Turn the dough out onto a floured surface and roll out to a 28 x 6 inch rectangle. Spread with the soft butter and sprinkle with the chopped sour cherries and brown sugar.

Roll up the dough from a long edge, so that it forms a thin log, and cut across into 16 even-size pieces. Lay the slices in the pan, cut sides up, cover loosely with oiled plastic wrap and allow to rise in a warm place for about 1 hour until the dough has risen slightly. Bake in a preheated oven, 425°F, for about 25 minutes until risen and golden. Leave for 5 minutes then lift out of the pan and cool on a wire rack. Mix the syrup with the lemon juice and use to glaze the slices.

For cardamom & apricot buns, crush 12 cardamom pods until the shells have split to release the seeds. Discard the shells and crush the seeds until coarsely ground. Make the dough as above, using orange zest instead of lemon, crushed cardamom instead of almond extract, and plump dried apricots instead of cherries, and shape as before. To make the icing mix ½ cup sifted confectioners' sugar with 1 ½ teaspoons orange juice and the seeds of 5 crushed cardamom pods.

real chocolate brownies

Makes **10**
Preparation time **15 minutes**
Cooking time **25 minutes**

1/3 cup **unsalted butter**, plus
    extra for greasing
3 oz **bittersweet chocolate**
2 **eggs**
1 cup **superfine sugar**
1 cup **all-purpose flour**
1/2 teaspoon **baking powder**

Grease an 8 inch square pan and line the base with nonstick parchment paper.

Melt the butter and chocolate together in a saucepan over a low heat. Beat the eggs and sugar together in a bowl until the mixture is pale and creamy. Stir the melted chocolate mixture into the egg mixture. Sift in the flour and baking powder and fold together. Turn the mixture into the pan and level the surface.

Bake in a preheated oven, 375°F, for 25 minutes until the brownies are firm on top and a skewer inserted into the center comes out clean. Cool in the pan for 5 minutes, then cut into squares.

For rich chocolate mocha brownies, roughly chop 1 cup pecan nuts. Dissolve 2 teaspoons espresso coffee powder in 1 tablespoon hot water. Chop 4 oz milk chocolate into small pieces. Make the brownies as above, adding the coffee to the melted chocolate and butter. Turn into the pan and sprinkle with the chopped chocolate and nuts before baking as above.

pastries

soft fruit tartlets

Makes **10–12**
Preparation time **30 minutes**,
  plus chilling and cooling
Cooking time **30 minutes**

1 cup **all-purpose flour**, sifted
5 tablespoons **chilled
  unsalted butter**, diced
½ cup **confectioners' sugar**,
  sifted, plus extra for dusting
  (optional)
3 **egg yolks**
3 teaspoons **cold water**
1 cup **heavy cream**
1 teaspoon **vanilla bean
  paste**
3 tablespoons **superfine
  sugar**
2 cups small **strawberries,
  raspberries**, and **red
  currants**
4 tablespoons **red currant
  jelly**

Put the flour and butter in a food processor and blend
until the mixture resembles bread crumbs. Add the
confectioners' sugar and blend briefly to mix. Add 1 of
the egg yolks and 1 teaspoon of the measurement water
and mix to a soft dough. Wrap in plastic wrap and chill for
at least 1 hour.

Divide the dough into 10–12 balls and push each into
push into the base of each hole of a 12-hole mini muffin
or tartlet pan, each with a capacity of about ¼ cup. Use
lightly floured fingers to press the dough up the sides of
sections, trimming off the excess around the tops with a
knife. Chill for 30 minutes. Line with nonstick parchment
paper and fill with pie weights. Bake in a preheated oven,
400°F, for 15 minutes. Remove from the oven and lift out
the weights and paper. Reduce the oven temperature to
325°F.

Beat together the cream, remaining egg yolks, vanilla
bean paste, and superfine sugar and pour into the shells.
Bake for about 15 minutes until the filling is lightly set.
Allow to cool in the pans before removing. Pile the fruits
on top of the pastries. Melt the red currant jelly in a small
saucepan with the remaining water until smooth and
syrupy. Use to glaze the tartlets.

For maple & walnut tartlets, make the dough as
above, adding ½ teaspoon ground pumpkin pie spice.
Press into the pan sections, making a dip in the center
of each rather than pressing it right up the sides of the
holes. Roughly chop ¾ cup pecan nuts and push into the
pastries. Drizzle each with ½ teaspoon maple syrup and
bake at 350°F, for 20 minutes until golden. Remove to a
wire rack to cool. Serve drizzled with a little maple syrup.

almond praline buns

Makes **16**
Preparation time **30 minutes**,
plus cooling
Cooking time **30 minutes**

4 tablespoons **chilled
unsalted butter**, diced
¾ cup **all-purpose flour**,
sifted
5 tablespoons **milk**
2 **eggs**, beaten
⅓ cup **slivered almonds**
2 tablespoons **superfine
sugar**
⅔ cup **heavy cream**
2 tablespoons **almond liqueur**
confectioners' sugar, for
dusting

Place 16 mini silicone muffin cups on a baking sheet.
Put the butter in a small saucepan with the milk and 5
tablespoons water. Heat gently until the butter dissolves.
Bring to a boil and remove from the heat. Immediately
tip in the flour and beat well until the mixture forms a
smooth ball that leaves the sides of the pan. Allow to cool
for 2 minutes. Gradually beat the eggs into the paste,
until smooth and glossy. Push a teaspoonful of the choux
pastry into a muffin cup. Fill the remainder in the same
way. Crumble 2 tablespoons of almonds over.

Bake in a preheated oven, 400°F, for about 20 minutes
until risen and golden. Remove from the oven, take out
of the cups, and make a small horizontal slit in the side
of each bun. Return to the oven for 3 minutes more.
Transfer to a wire rack to cool. Sprinkle the remaining
almonds onto a baking sheet lined with nonstick
parchment paper and sprinkle the superfine sugar on
top. Place under a moderate broiler, watching closely, for
5 minutes until the sugar starts to caramelize. Allow to
cool. Blend the mixture in a food processor and blend
until finely ground. Whip the cream with the liqueur until
holding its shape. Stir in the ground praline and spoon
into the pastries. Serve dusted with confectioners' sugar.

For crème pâtissière buns, make and bake the buns
as above. Put ⅔ cup light cream in a saucepan with 1
teaspoon vanilla extract and bring to a boil. Beat together
2 egg yolks, 1½ tablespoons superfine sugar and 1
tablespoon all-purpose flour in a bowl. Beat in the hot
cream. Return to the saucepan and cook over a gentle
heat, stirring until thickened. Turn into a bowl, cover with
waxed paper to prevent a skin forming and allow to cool.
Use to fill the buns.

pineapple & rum puffs

Makes **25**
Preparation time **30 minutes**,
 plus cooling
Cooking time **20 minutes**

½ juicy ripe **pineapple**
⅓ cup **raisins**
3 tablespoons **honey**
4 tablespoons **rum**
butter, for greasing
1 lb ready-made **puff pastry**
flour, for dusting
1 **egg** yolk
¾ cup **mascarpone cheese**
2 tablespoons **confectioners'
 sugar**, sifted

Cut away the skin from the pineapple and cut the flesh into thin slices. Chop the pineapple into small pieces, discarding the central core. Put in a bowl and stir in the raisins, 2 tablespoons of the honey, and 2 tablespoons of the rum.

Grease a baking sheet. Roll out the pastry on a lightly floured surface to an 11 inch square. Trim off the edges and cut the pastry into 5 even-size strips. Cut across in the opposite direction to make squares. Using the tip of a sharp knife, make a shallow cut, ½ inch away from the edges to make a rim. Beat the egg yolk with the remaining honey and use to brush over the pastry rims.

Bake in a preheated oven, 425°F, for 15 minutes, or until risen and golden. Scoop out the centers of the pastries to shape containers and return to the oven for 5 minutes. Transfer to a wire rack to cool.

Beat the mascarpone with the confectioners' sugar and remaining rum and spoon into the shells. Pile the pineapple mixture on top to serve.

For rhubarb & orange puffs, cut 10 oz young rhubarb into ½ inch pieces and put in a saucepan with ½ cup superfine sugar and the finely grated zest and juice of 1 orange. Cook gently until the rhubarb is just tender. Drain the rhubarb into a bowl. Mix 1 teaspoon cornstarch with 1 tablespoon water and add to the juices in the pan. Cook, stirring until thickened. Add to the rhubarb and allow to cool. Make and cook the pastry shells as above. Beat 2 tablespoons sifted confectioners' sugar into ¾ cup cream cheese and spoon into the shells. Pile the rhubarb on top to serve.

chocolate éclairs & cream liqueur

Makes **18**
Preparation time **40 minutes**,
  plus cooling
Cooking time **15 minutes**

¼ cup **unsalted butter**, plus
  extra for greasing
⅔ cup **water**
10 tablespoons **all-purpose
  flour**, sifted
2 **eggs**, beaten
½ teaspoon **vanilla extract**

Filling
1 cup **heavy cream**
2 tablespoons **confectioners'
  sugar**
4 tablespoons **whiskey** or
  coffee cream liqueur

Topping
2 tablespoons **unsalted butter**
4 oz **bittersweet chocolate**,
  broken into pieces
1 tablespoon **confectioners'
  sugar**
2–3 teaspoons **milk**

Grease a large baking sheet. Heat the butter and measurement water gently in a saucepan until melted. Bring to a boil, then add the flour all at once and beat the mixture until it forms a smooth ball that leaves the sides of the pan clean. Allow to cool for 2 minutes.

Beat the eggs and vanilla extract into the paste gradually until thick and smooth. Spoon the choux pastry into a large pastry bag fitted with a ½ inch plain piping tip, and pipe 7 cm (3 inch) lines of pastry onto the baking sheet.

Bake in a preheated oven, 400°F, for 15 minutes until well risen. Make a slit in the side of each éclair for the steam to escape then return to the turned-off oven for 5 minutes. Allow to cool.

Whip the cream for the filling to soft swirls, then gradually beat in the confectioners' sugar and liqueur. Slit each éclair lengthwise and spoon or pipe in the cream.

Make the chocolate topping by heating the butter, chocolate, and confectioners' sugar together gently until just melted. Stir in the milk, then spoon over the top of the éclairs. Serve on the day.

For citrus iced buns, make and bake the éclairs as above. Make the filling, replacing the whiskey or coffee liqueur with an orange-flavored liqueur or freshly squeezed orange juice. Use to fill the buns. Put 1¾ cups fondant icing sugar in a bowl and stir in enough lemon juice to make an icing that thickly coats the back of the spoon. Add a drop of natural yellow food coloring if desired. Spoon over the top of the éclairs.

plum tripiti

Makes **24**

Preparation time **40 minutes**

Cooking time **10 minutes**

⅓ cup **unsalted butter**, melted

4 oz **feta cheese**, drained and coarsely grated

6 tablespoons **ricotta cheese**

¼ cup **superfine sugar**

¼ teaspoon **ground cinnamon**

1 **egg**, beaten

12 sheets of **phyllo pastry**

flour, for dusting

1 lb small **red plums**, halved and pitted

confectioners' sugar, for dusting

Grease a baking sheet with some of the melted butter. Mix the feta, ricotta, sugar, cinnamon, and egg in a bowl.

Unfold the pastry sheets on a lightly floured surface, then put one in front of you, with a short side facing you (covering the others with plastic wrap). Brush the pastry sheet with a little of the melted butter, then cut in half to make 2 long strips.

Place a spoonful of the cheese mixture a little up from the bottom left-hand corner of each strip, then cover with a plum half. Fold the bottom right-hand corner of one strip diagonally over the plum to cover the filling and to make a triangle. Fold the bottom left-hand corner upward to make a second triangle, then keep folding until the top of the strip is reached and the filling is enclosed in a triangle of pastry. Place on the baking sheet and repeat until 24 triangles have been made using all the filling. Brush the outside of the triangles with the remaining butter.

Bake in a preheated oven, 400°F, for about 10 minutes until the pastry is golden and the plum juices begin to run from the sides. Dust with sifted confectioners' sugar and allow to cool for 15 minutes before serving.

For pear & cream cheese triangles, make the filling as above, using 6 tablespoons cream cheese to replace the feta and adding 1 teaspoon vanilla bean paste with the cinnamon. Peel, core, and dice 3 ripe juicy pears and toss with 2 teaspoons lemon juice to prevent them from browning. Assemble the pastries, spooning the diced pears onto the cream cheese mixture. Dust with superfine sugar and serve warm or cold.

tangy lemon squares

Makes **16**
Preparation time **25 minutes**,
  plus chilling and cooling
Cooking time **45 minutes**

1 cup **all-purpose flour**,
  sifted, plus extra for dusting
¼ lb plus 4 tablespoons (1½
  sticks) **chilled unsalted
  butter**, diced
6 tablespoons **confectioners'
  sugar**, sifted, plus extra for
  dusting
1 teaspoon **cold water**
6 **eggs**, beaten, and 1 **egg
  yolk**
1¼ cups **superfine sugar**
finely grated zest and juice of
  4 **lemons**

Put the flour and 4 tablespoons of the butter in a food
processor and blend until the mixture resembles bread
crumbs. Add the confectioners' sugar, measurement
water, and egg yolk and blend to make a soft dough.
Wrap in plastic wrap and chill for at least 30 minutes.

Roll out the dough thinly on a lightly floured surface to
an 8½ inch square. Fit into an 8 inch square removable-
bottomed cake pan or shallow baking pan, pressing
the pastry down firmly around the edges. Bake in a
preheated oven, 400°F, for 15 minutes. Remove from
the oven and reduce the oven temperature to 350°F.

Put the whole eggs, superfine sugar, and remaining
butter into a saucepan and heat very gently until the
sugar has dissolved. Stir in the lemon zest and juice and
cook, stirring, for 5–10 minutes until the mixture has
thickened slightly. Strain through a sieve into a pitcher
and pour over the pastry. Bake for 20 minutes until just
set. Allow to cool completely in the pan. Transfer to a
plate. Dust with confectioners' sugar and cut into
16 squares.

For meringue-frosted lime squares, prepare and
bake the pastry as above. Make the filling, replacing
3 of the lemons and the lemon zest with the zest and
juice of 4 limes. Bake and allow to cool. Put 2 egg
whites, 1 cup sifted confectioners' sugar, and a pinch of
cream of tartar into a thoroughly clean heatproof bowl
and rest it over a pan of gently simmering water. Beat
with a hand-held electric mixer until thickened. Remove
from the heat and beat for an additional 2–3 minutes
until softly peaking. Use a spatula to spread the frosting
over the filling.

honey, grape, & cinnamon tartlets

Makes **16**
Preparation time **25 minutes**
Cooking time **10 minutes**

¾ cup **seedless red grapes**, peeled and halved
¾ cup **seedless white grapes**, peeled and halved
3 tablespoons **dessert wine** or **grape juice**
2 tablespoons **unsalted butter**, melted
½ teaspoon **ground cinnamon**
3 sheets of **phyllo pastry**
flour, for dusting
6 tablespoons **heavy cream**
6 tablespoons **plain whole milk yogurt**
2 tablespoons **honey**, plus extra to drizzle

Place 16 mini silicone muffin cups on a baking sheet.

Put the grapes in a bowl with the wine or grape juice. Mix the melted butter with the cinnamon.

Unfold the pastry sheets on a lightly floured surface, then put one in front of you (covering the others with plastic wrap) cut into 2¾ inch squares. Brush the squares lightly with the spiced butter. Cut out more squares from the other 2 sheets and position over the first, adjusting the positions so the points are evenly staggered. Press into the cups and brush with a little more butter.

Bake in a preheated oven, 375°F, for 10 minutes until golden. Remove from the oven and transfer to a wire rack to cool.

Beat the cream with the yogurt and honey until just holding its shape. Drain the grapes over the cream so you can beat the juice into the cream. Spoon the cream mixture into the pastry shells and pile the grapes on top. Serve drizzled with extra honey.

For blueberry & cream cheese tartlets, make the phyllo shells as above, omitting the cinnamon from the butter. Beat 1 cup cream cheese in a bowl with 1 teaspoon vanilla bean paste and 2 tablespoons sifted confectioners' sugar until smooth. Spoon into the shells and top with blueberry preserves. Serve lightly dusted with confectioners' sugar.

churros

Makes **12**
Preparation time **20 minutes**,
  plus cooling
Cooking time **10 minutes**

1¾ cups **all-purpose flour**
¼ teaspoon **salt**
5 tablespoons **superfine sugar**
1 cup plus 2 tablespoons **water**
1 **egg**, beaten, plus 1 **egg yolk**
1 teaspoon **vanilla extract**
4 cups **sunflower oil**
1 teaspoon **ground cinnamon**

Mix the flour, salt, and 1 tablespoon of the sugar in a bowl. Pour the measurement water into a saucepan and bring to a boil. Take off the heat, add the flour mixture, and beat well. Then return to the heat and stir until it forms a smooth ball that leaves the sides of the pan clean. Remove from the heat and cool for 10 minutes.

Gradually beat the whole egg, egg yolk, and vanilla extract into the flour mixture until smooth. Spoon into a large pastry bag fitted with a ½ inch plain tip. Pour the oil into a medium saucepan to a depth of 1 inch. Heat to 340°F on a candy thermometer. Alternatively, to test if the oil is hot enough, pipe a tiny amount of the mixture into the oil: if the oil bubbles instantly, it is ready to use. Pipe coils, S-shapes, and squiggly lines into the oil, in small batches, cutting the ends off at the tip with kitchen scissors. Cook the churros for 2–3 minutes until they float and are golden, turning, to brown evenly.

Lift the churros out of the oil, drain well on paper towels then sprinkle with the remaining sugar mixed with the cinnamon. Continue piping and frying until all the mixture has been used (probably 3 batches). Serve warm or cold.

For white chocolate sauce, put 1 tablespoon superfine sugar in a small saucepan with ½ teaspoon ground ginger and 5 tablespoons water and heat gently until the sugar dissolves. Bring to a boil and remove from the heat. Add 5 oz chopped white chocolate and leave until melted, stirring frequently until smooth. Stir in 5 tablespoons heavy cream. Make the churros as above, but instead of dusting with the spiced sugar, serve with the sauce for dipping.

citrus baklava

Makes **24**
Preparation time **30 minutes**,
plus chilling
Cooking time **35 minutes**

13 oz package **phyllo pastry**
flour, for dusting
½ cup **unsalted butter**,
melted

Filling
⅔ cup **walnut** pieces
1 cup shelled **pistachio nuts**,
plus some slivers to decorate
⅔ cup **blanched almonds**
⅓ cup **superfine sugar**
½ teaspoon **ground**
cinnamon

Syrup
1 **lemon**
1 small **orange**
2 cups **superfine sugar**
pinch of **ground cinnamon**
⅔ cup **water**

Make the filling by dry-frying the nuts in a nonstick pan for 3–4 minutes, stirring until light brown. Allow to cool slightly, chop roughly, and mix with the sugar and cinnamon. Unfold the pastry on a lightly floured surface and cut it into rectangles the same size as the base of a 7 x 11 inch small roasting pan. Wrap half the pastry in plastic wrap so that it doesn't dry out. Brush each sheet of pastry with melted butter, then layer up in the roasting pan. Spoon in the nut mixture, then unwrap and cover with the remaining pastry, buttering layers as you go.

Cut the pastry into 6 squares, then cut each square into 4 triangles. Bake in a preheated oven, 350°F, for 30–35 minutes, covering with foil after 20 minutes to prevent it overbrowning. Meanwhile, make the syrup. Pare the peel off the citrus fruits with a zester or vegetable peeler, then cut the peel into strips. Squeeze the juice. Put the strips and juice in a saucepan with the sugar, cinnamon, and measurement water. Heat gently until the sugar dissolves, then simmer for 5 minutes without stirring.

Pour the hot syrup over the pastry as soon as it comes out of the oven. Allow to cool, then chill for 3 hours. Remove from the pan and arrange the pieces on a serving plate, sprinkled with slivers of pistachio. Store in the refrigerator for up to 2 days.

For baklava with spices, bake the baklava as above. Make the syrup, adding 1 teaspoon coriander seeds crushed with a mortar and pestle, ¼ teaspoon ground cloves, and 1 teaspoon rose water or orange flower water with the citrus fruit juice. Pour over the cooked baklava and finish as above.

blackberry & apple vol au vents

Makes **20**
Preparation time **15 minutes**
Cooking time about **15
minutes**

1/3 cup **unsalted butter**
1/3 cup **superfine sugar**
2 small, crisp **dessert apples**
1 1/2 cups small **blackberries**
1 teaspoon **vanilla bean
paste**
2 teaspoons **lemon juice**
20 **vol au vent shells**
confectioners' sugar, for
dusting

Melt the butter in a skillet and stir in the sugar. Cook over a gentle heat until the sugar dissolves. Continue to cook until the mixture starts to caramelize. Remove from the heat.

Peel, core, and chop the apples into the pan and cook gently for 3–5 minutes until the apples start to soften. Add the blackberries and cook for 1 minute more. Stir in the vanilla bean paste and lemon juice.

Spoon into the vol au vent shells, packing the mixture down gently. Place on a baking sheet and cook in a preheated oven, 350°F, for 5 minutes to warm through.

Reduce the syrup left in the skillet for about 5 minutes, until thickened, then spoon onto the fruits. Lightly dust with confectioners' sugar and serve decorated with mint sprigs or edible flowers.

For homemade vol au vent shells, roll out 1 lb puff pastry until a generous 1/4 inch thick. Cut out circles using a 2 inch round cutter and space slightly apart on a greased baking sheet. Layer up the trimmings and reroll to cut more circles. Using a 1 3/4 inch round cutter, impress circles in the centers of the pastries, but don't press right through to the baking sheet. Lift away the cutter. Brush the top edges of the circles only with egg yolk to glaze, and bake in a preheated oven, 425°F, for 12 minutes until golden and well risen. Remove from the oven and lift out the risen pastry in the centers to leave shells. Return to the oven for 5 minutes more. Once completely cool, store in an airtight container for up to 2 days.

gingered profiteroles

Serves **4**
Preparation time **35 minutes**,
  plus cooling
Cooking time **20 minutes**

¼ cup **unsalted butter**, plus
  extra for greasing
⅔ cup **water**
pinch of **salt**
10 tablespoons **all-purpose
  flour**, sifted
2 **eggs**
½ teaspoon **vanilla extract**
1 cup **heavy cream**
⅓ cup finely chopped
  crystallized or **candied
  ginger**

Sauce
5 oz **bittersweet chocolate**,
  broken into pieces
⅔ cup **milk**
¼ cup **superfine sugar**
2 tablespoons **brandy**

Grease a large baking sheet. Pour the measurement water into a medium saucepan, add the butter and salt and heat until the butter has melted. Bring up to a boil, then take off the heat and stir in the flour. Put the pan back on the heat and cook briefly, stirring until the mixture makes a smooth ball. Allow to cool.

Beat the eggs and vanilla extract together, then gradually beat into the flour mixture until smooth. Spoon the mixture into a large pastry bag fitted with a ¾ inch plain piping tip, and pipe 20 balls onto the baking sheet, leaving space in between.

Bake in a preheated oven, 400°F, for 15 minutes until well risen. Make a slit in the side of each ball for the steam to escape, return to the turned-off oven for 5 minutes, then take out and cool. Make the sauce by heating the chocolate, milk, and sugar in a saucepan and stirring until smooth. Take off the heat and mix in the brandy. Whip the cream until it forms soft peaks, then fold in the ginger. Enlarge the slit in each profiterole and spoon in the ginger cream. Pile into serving dishes and drizzle with the reheated sauce.

For feathered chocolate profiteroles, make and bake the profiteroles as above. Whip 1 cup heavy cream with 1 tablespoon confectioners' sugar and use to fill the profiteroles. Melt 5 oz bittersweet chocolate and 2 oz white chocolate in separate bowls (see page 14). Spoon a little bittersweet chocolate over the top of a profiterole and drizzle a little white chocolate over the top. Swirl the two chocolates together with the tip of a skewer to feather. Repeat with the remainder.

orange puffs

Makes **25**
Preparation time **25 minutes**
Cooking time **12 minutes**

butter, for greasing
8 oz prepared **puff pastry**
flour, for dusting
2 tablespoons **superfine sugar**
finely grated zest of 1 **orange**
1 **egg yolk**

Buttercream
¼ cup **unsalted butter**, softened
¾ cup **confectioners' sugar**, sifted, plus extra for dusting (optional)
1 tablespoon **orange juice**
1 tablespoon **lemon juice**

Grease a baking sheet. Roll out the pastry on a lightly floured surface to a 9 inch square and cut in half. Mix 1 tablespoon of the superfine sugar with the orange zest and sprinkle over one half of the pastry. Lay the other half on top and reroll the pastry to a 10 inch square. Trim off the edges to neaten.

Cut the pastry into 5 strips, then across in the opposite direction to make 25 squares. Transfer to the baking sheet, spacing them slightly apart, and prick all over with a fork. Bake in a preheated oven, 400°F, for 10 minutes until risen and pale golden.

Beat the egg yolk with the remaining superfine sugar. Brush over the pastries and return to the oven for an additional 2 minutes or until golden. Transfer to a wire rack to cool.

Make the buttercream by beating together the butter, confectioners' sugar, and orange and lemon juice. Split each pastry in half and sandwich with the buttercream. Dust lightly with confectioners' sugar, if desired.

For cinnamon fruit puffs, thinly roll out 10 oz puff pastry on a lightly floured surface and cut in half. Mix 2 tablespoons superfine sugar with 1 teaspoon ground cinnamon and sprinkle over one half. Sprinkle with ½ cup currants. Lay the second sheet of pastry on top of the first and reroll until thin enough for the raisins to show through clearly. Transfer to a greased baking sheet and cut into rectangles measuring about 3 x 1¾ inches. Brush with beaten egg and dust with superfine sugar. Bake in a preheated oven, 400°F, for about 15 minutes until golden. Transfer to a wire rack to cool.

chocolate phyllo twiglets

Makes **22**
Preparation time **20 minutes**
Cooking time **10 minutes**

¼ cup **unsalted butter**,
 melted, plus extra for
 greasing
½ cup chopped **bittersweet**
 or **milk chocolate**
3 tablespoons **hazelnuts**,
 toasted and chopped
2 tablespoons **raisins**,
 chopped
4 sheets of **phyllo pastry**
flour, for dusting
¼ cup **superfine sugar**
½ teaspoon **ground**
 cinnamon

Grease a baking sheet.

Mix together the chocolate, hazelnuts, and raisins.

Unfold the pastry sheets on a lightly floured surface, then put one in front of you (covering the others with plastic wrap) and brush with a little of the melted butter. Place a second sheet on top. Cut the pastry into 5 x 2½ inch rectangles.

Sprinkle a heaping teaspoonful of the chocolate mixture in a line down the long edge of one strip, leaving a ½ inch area uncovered at either end. Fold the ends over the chocolate, then roll up, starting from the chocolate-covered side. Shape the remainder in the same way using the other sheets of phyllo, so that you have 22 in all. Brush the pastries with more butter.

Bake in a preheated oven, 425°F, for about 10 minutes until deep golden.

Mix the sugar with the cinnamon and place on a plate. Roll the warm pastries in the spiced sugar until coated. Serve warm or transfer to a wire rack to cool.

For date & fresh ginger sticks, finely chop 1 cup dates and mix in a bowl with 1 tablespoon finely chopped fresh ginger and 1 tablespoon honey. Use this mixture to fill the phyllo pastries, then bake as above. After baking, roll the pastries in the spiced sugar, using ground ginger instead of the cinnamon.

mini nectarine & blueberry tarts

Makes **12**

Preparation time **15 minutes**

Cooking time **8 minutes**

2 tablespoons **unsalted butter**

2 teaspoons **olive oil**

4 sheets of **phyllo pastry**

flour, for dusting

2 tablespoons **red berry jelly**

juice of ½ **orange**

4 ripe **nectarines**, halved,
   pitted, and sliced

1¼ cups **blueberries**

confectioners' sugar, for
   dusting

Heat the butter and oil in a small saucepan until the butter has melted.

Unfold the pastry on a lightly floured surface and separate into sheets. Brush lightly with the butter mixture, then cut into 24 pieces, each 4 x 3½ inches.

Arrange a piece in each of the sections of a deep 12-hole muffin pan, then add a second piece at a slight angle to the first pieces to give a pretty jagged edge to each pastry shell.

Bake in a preheated oven, 350°F, for 6–8 minutes until golden. Meanwhile, warm the jelly and orange juice in a saucepan, then add the nectarines and blueberries and warm through.

Lift the tart shells carefully out of the muffin pan and transfer to a serving dish. Fill the shells with the warm fruits and dust with sifted confectioners' sugar. Serve with cream or ice cream.

For mascarpone & vanilla ice cream, put 1 cup superfine sugar in a saucepan with 2 cups water and heat gently until the sugar dissolves. Bring to a boil and boil for 3 minutes. Remove from the heat, stir in 2 tablespoons lemon juice, and allow to cool. Beat 2 cups mascarpone cheese in a bowl with 2 teaspoons vanilla bean paste. Gradually beat in the cooled syrup. Churn in an ice cream machine and transfer to a freezer container. Freeze until ready to use. Serve scooped over the tarts.

spicy raisin palmiers

Makes **22**
Preparation time **15 minutes**,
   plus freezing
Cooking time **12 minutes**

butter, for greasing
½ cup **raisins**, chopped
1 teaspoon **ground pumpkin
   pie spice**
2 tablespoons **superfine
   sugar**
8 oz prepared **puff pastry**
flour, for dusting
1 **egg yolk**
1 teaspoon **water**

To serve
vanilla ice cream
Pedro Ximenez sherry, or any
   other **sweet, well-flavored
   sherry**

Grease 2 baking sheets.

Mix together the raisins, spice, and sugar. Roll out the pastry on a lightly floured surface to a 12 x 8 inch rectangle. Mix the egg yolk with the measurement water and brush some of it sparingly over the pastry, taking it right to the edges. Sprinkle with the raisin mixture. Roll up the pastry, starting from a long side, to shape a neat log. Wrap in plastic wrap and freeze for 30 minutes.

Trim off the ends from the pastry log. Using a sharp knife, cut across into 22 slices, ½ inch wide. Roll lightly with a floured rolling pin to flatten slightly, then transfer to the baking sheets. Brush with the remaining egg yolk.

Bake in a preheated oven, 425°F, for about 12 minutes until risen and golden. Serve warm or transfer to a wire rack and allow to cool a little or completely,.

Place a small scoop of vanilla ice cream onto each palmier. (A melon baller is ideal, but if you don't have one, use a teaspoon.) Drizzle with a little sherry to serve.

For mocha cream palmiers, blend 2 teaspoons espresso coffee powder with 2 teaspoons unsweetened cocoa powder and 2 tablespoons vanilla sugar (see page 168). Make the pastries as above, using the coffee mixture instead of the raisin one. Bake as above. Melt 4 oz bittersweet chocolate (see page 14), and stir in 4 tablespoons heavy cream. Once the chocolate cream is cold but not set, use it to sandwich the pastries together.

papaya, lime & mango tartlets

Makes **20**
Preparation time **35 minutes**,
  plus chilling
Cooking time **20 minutes**

8 oz **chilled sweet shortcrust
  pastry**
flour, for dusting
thinly grated zest and juice of 2
  large, juicy **limes**
6 tablespoons **heavy cream**
2/3 cup **full-fat condensed
  milk**
2 tablespoons finely diced
  mango
2 tablespoons finely diced
  papaya
lime zest, to decorate

Roll out the pastry on a lightly floured surface to 1/8 inch thick, then, using a 2 inch round cookie or pastry cutter, stamp out 20 rounds.

Use the pastry rounds to line 20 sections of 2 x 12-hole mini tartlet pans. Prick the pastry bases with a fork. Line the cases with nonstick parchment paper and fill with pie weights. Bake blind in a preheated oven, 375°F, for 10 minutes, then remove the paper and weights and return the shells to the oven for 5–10 minutes, or until they are crisp and golden. Remove from the oven and allow to cool in the tins.

Put the lime zest in a blender with the cream and condensed milk and pulse until well combined. With the motor running, slowly pour in the lime juice and process until blended. (Alternatively, mix well by hand.) Transfer to a bowl, cover, and chill in the refrigerator for 3–4 hours or until firm.

Put the tartlet shells on a serving platter and spoon the lime mixture into each shell. Mix the mango with the papaya and, using a teaspoon, top the shells with the fruit mixture. Decorate with lime zest and serve immediately.

For raspberry cream tartlets, make the tartlet shells and filling as above. Spoon the filling into the shells. Warm 4 tablespoons raspberry jelly in a saucepan with the grated zest and juice of 1 lime. Cook for 1 minute until syrupy, then press through a strainer into a small bowl. Pile 2½ cups fresh raspberries onto the tartlets and drizzle with the syrup. Dust lightly with confectioners' sugar.

meringues &
macaroons

brown sugar meringues

Makes **24**
Preparation time **25 minutes**,
  plus cooling
Cooking time **45 minutes**

butter, for greasing
5 tablespoons **light brown
  sugar**
¼ cup **superfine sugar**
2 **egg whites**
1 cup **mascarpone cheese**
2 tablespoons **milk**
2 tablespoons **confectioners'
  sugar**, sifted
1 teaspoon **vanilla bean
  paste**

Grease 2 baking sheets and line with nonstick parchment paper. Mix the 2 sugars together.

Beat the egg whites in a thoroughly clean bowl until stiffly peaking. Gradually beat in the sugars, a dessertspoonful at a time and beating well between each addition, until the mixture is stiff and glossy.

Spoon into a large pastry bag fitted with a ½ inch star tip. Pipe 24 fingers, 2½ inches long onto the baking sheets, leaving a small space between each.

Bake in a preheated oven, 350°F, for about 45 minutes until crisp, rotating the baking sheets halfway through cooking. Transfer to a wire rack to cool.

Beat the mascarpone in a bowl with the confectioners' sugar, milk, and vanilla bean paste until smooth. Turn into a small bowl. Serve with the meringue fingers for dipping.

For pistachio & white chocolate meringues, remove the skins from ½ cup shelled pistachio nuts (see page 70). Drain the nuts and sprinkle between plenty of sheets of paper towel. Rub under the palm of your hand to remove the skins from the nuts. Any skins that still won't come away easily can be peeled away. Finely chop the nuts. Make the meringues as above, using extra superfine sugar to replace the brown sugar. Sprinkle with the nuts before baking. Very gently heat 6 tablespoons heavy cream in a small saucepan with ½ cup chopped white chocolate until hot but not boiling. Remove from the heat and leave until the chocolate has melted. Allow to cool completely, then use to sandwich the fingers together.

red currant meringue cupcakes

Makes **16**
Preparation time **30 minutes**,
  plus cooling
Cooking time **20 minutes**

¼ cup **lightly salted butter**,
  softened
¾ cup **superfine sugar**
½ cup **self-rising flour**, sifted
1 **egg**
1 piece of **preserved stem
  ginger in syrup**, finely
  chopped
3 tablespoons **red currant
  jelly**
2 teaspoons **water**
¾ cup **red currants**, plus extra
  sprigs to decorate
2 **egg whites**

Place 16 mini silicone muffin cups on a baking sheet.
Put the butter, ¼ cup of the sugar, the flour, egg, and
ginger in a bowl and beat with a hand-held electric
mixer until light and creamy. Divide between the cups.

Bake in a preheated oven, 350°F, for 10–12 minutes
until risen and just firm. Allow to cool in the cups for
2 minutes before transferring to a wire rack to cool
completely. Raise the oven temperature to 450°F.

Heat the red currant jelly in a small saucepan with the
measurement water until the jelly softens. Add the red
currants and cook gently for 5 minutes to soften. Allow
to cool.

Use a teaspoon to scoop out the centers of the
cupcakes to make a cavity. Spoon the red currant
mixture into the centers.

Beat the egg whites in a thoroughly clean bowl until
stiffly peaking. Gradually beat in the remaining sugar,
a dessertspoonful at a time and beating well between
each addition, until the mixture is stiff and glossy. Pile
the meringue onto the cakes and swirl with a spatula.
Return to the baking sheet and bake for about 2
minutes, watching closely, until the meringue peaks are
turning deep brown. Serve warm or cold decorated with
small red currant sprigs.

For lemon meringue cupcakes, make the cakes as
above, replacing the ginger with the finely grated zest
of 1 lemon. Once cooled, scoop out the centers with
a teaspoon and fill with a teaspoonful of lemon curd.
Make the meringue and finish as above.

mini chocolate meringues

Makes **36**
Preparation time **15 minutes**,
  plus cooling
Cooking time 1¼ **hours**

butter, for greasing
3 **egg whites**
⅓ cup **superfine sugar**
⅓ cup **light brown sugar**
6 tablespoons grated **milk
  chocolate**

Grease 2 baking sheets and line with nonstick parchment paper.

Beat the egg whites in a thoroughly clean bowl until stiffly peaking. Beat in the superfine sugar 1 tablespoon at a time, then beat in the light brown sugar, also 1 tablespoon at a time. Fold in the chocolate. Drop teaspoonfuls of the meringue mixture onto the baking sheets.

Bake in a preheated oven, 275°F, for 1¼ hours, then turn off the heat and leave in the oven for another 30 minutes. Once cooled, gently peel away the paper from the meringues and store in an airtight container for up to 3 days.

For white chocolate & mint disks, make up the meringue as above, but use ⅔ cup superfine sugar instead of the mixed superfine and brown sugar. Fold in 6 tablespoons grated white chocolate in place of the milk chocolate and add 1 teaspoon mint extract. Place about 36 teaspoonfuls of the mixture on the baking sheets and spread with the back of the spoon to make shallow disks about ¼ inch thick. Bake as above.

baby passion fruit pavlovas

Makes **20**
Preparation time **30 minutes**,
    plus cooling
Cooking time **1 hour**

butter, for greasing
3 **egg whites**
¾ cup **superfine sugar**
1 teaspoon **white wine
    vinegar**
1 teaspoon **cornstarch**
6 **passion fruit**
⅔ cup **heavy cream**
6 tablespoons **plain whole
    milk yogurt**
20 cape **gooseberries**

Grease and line 2 baking sheets with nonstick parchment paper. Beat the egg whites in a thoroughly clean bowl until stiffly peaking. Gradually beat in the sugar, a dessertspoonful at a time and beating well between each addition, until the mixture is stiff and glossy. Drizzle the vinegar into the bowl and sift in the cornstarch. Stir gently.

Place 20 spoonfuls of the mixture, each about the size of a golf ball, on the lined baking sheets and flatten into a neat dome shape with a spatula. Push a deep cavity into each center using the back of a teaspoon. Bake in a preheated oven, 325°F, for about 1 hour until the pavlovas feel crisp to the touch. Allow to cool on the baking sheets.

Scoop the pulp from 3 of the passion fruit and press through a strainer into a bowl. Add the cream and yogurt and beat with a hand-held electric mixer until softly peaking. Spoon into the meringue cases. Scoop the pulp from the remaining passion fruit and spoon over the tops. Decorate each pavlova with a cape gooseberry.

For strawberry & vanilla pavlovas, split a vanilla bean lengthwise and scoop out the seeds with the tip of the knife. (Halve the bean and put in a jar of superfine sugar for 2–3 weeks, stirring occasionally, to make homemade vanilla sugar.) Mash the seeds with 1 tablespoon superfine sugar to disperse the seeds evenly. Make the meringues as above, adding the spoonful of vanilla seed sugar with the rest of the sugar. Bake as above. Fill the meringues with ⅔ cup whipped heavy cream and sprinkle with small halved strawberries. Melt 3 tablespoons red currant jelly in a small saucepan with 2 teaspoons water until dissolved. Drizzle over the strawberries to glaze.

banoffee meringues

Makes **20**
Preparation time **30 minutes**,
  plus cooling and setting
Cooking time **1¼ hours**

butter, for greasing
3 **egg whites**
½ cup **light brown sugar**
⅓ cup **superfine sugar**
1 small ripe **banana**
1 tablespoon **lemon juice**
⅔ cup **heavy cream**
4 tablespoons **ready-made toffee fudge sauce**

Grease 2 baking sheets and line with nonstick parchment paper. Beat the egg whites in a thoroughly clean bowl until stiffly peaking. Gradually beat in the sugars, a teaspoonful at a time, until it has all been added. Beat for a few minutes more until the mixture is thick and glossy. Take a large teaspoonful of meringue and, using another spoon to scoop it off the first spoon, drop it onto the baking sheet to make an oval-shaped meringue. Continue until all the mixture has been used, making 40 meringues.

Bake in a preheated oven, 225°F, for 1–1¼ hours or until the meringues are firm and may be easily peeled off the paper. Allow to cool still on the sheets.

Mash the banana roughly with the lemon juice. Whip the cream until it forms soft peaks, then beat in 2 tablespoons of the toffee fudge sauce. Combine with the mashed banana, then use to sandwich the meringues together in pairs and arrange in paper bake cups. Drizzle with the remaining toffee fudge sauce and serve immediately. Unfilled meringues may be stored in an airtight container for up to 3 days.

For homemade toffee sauce, put 5 tablespoons water in a small heavy saucepan with 1 cup superfine sugar and heat gently until the sugar dissolves completely. Bring to a boil and boil until the syrup turns to a golden caramel color. Remove from the heat and dip the base of the pan in cold water to prevent further cooking. Add ¼ cup unsalted butter and ⅔ cup heavy cream and return to a gentle heat, stirring until the caramel has softened and the sauce becomes smooth. Allow to cool. This sauce may be refrigerated for up to 5 days.

pistachio & chocolate meringues

Makes **20**
Preparation time **30 minutes**,
 plus cooling and setting
Cooking time **1 hour**

butter, for greasing
3 **egg whites**
¾ cup **superfine sugar**
½ cup shelled **pistachio nuts**,
 finely chopped
5 oz **bittersweet chocolate**,
 broken into pieces
⅔ cup **heavy cream**

Grease and line 2 baking sheets with nonstick parchment paper.

Beat the egg whites in a thoroughly clean bowl until stiffly peaking. Gradually beat in the sugar, a teaspoonful at a time, until it has all been added. Beat for a few minutes more until the mixture is thick and glossy.

Fold in the pistachios, then spoon heaping teaspoonfuls of the mixture into rough swirly mounds on the baking sheets.

Bake in a preheated oven, 225°F, for 45–60 minutes, or until the meringues are firm and may be easily peeled off the paper. Allow to cool still on the paper.

Melt the chocolate (see page 14). Lift the meringues off the paper and dip the bases into the chocolate. Return to the paper, tilted on their sides, and leave in a cool place until the chocolate has hardened.

Whip the cream until just holding its shape, then use to sandwich the meringues together in pairs. Arrange in paper bake cups, if desired, on a cake plate or stand. Eat on the day they are filled. (Left plain, the meringues will keep in an airtight container for 3 days.)

For saffron meringues with clotted cream, make the meringues as above, omitting the pistachio nuts and crumbling ½ teaspoon saffron strands into the meringue mixture when you start adding the sugar. Place dessertspoonfuls of the mixture onto the baking sheet and bake as above. Serve with a bowl of clotted cream.

french macaroons

Makes **24**
Preparation time **20 minutes**,
 plus standing
Cooking time **10 minutes**

butter, for greasing
½ cup **confectioners' sugar**
9 tablespoons **ground almonds**
2 **egg whites**
½ cup **superfine sugar**
pink and **green food coloring**

Grease 2 baking sheets and line with nonstick parchment paper.

Put the confectioners' sugar in a food processor with the ground almonds and blend to a very fine consistency.

Put the egg whites in a thoroughly clean bowl and beat until stiffly peaking. Gradually beat in the superfine sugar, a tablespoonful at a time and beating well after each addition, until thick and very glossy. Divide the mixture equally between 2 bowls and add a few drops of food coloring to each bowl. Divide the almond mixture equally between the 2 bowls and use a metal spoon to stir the mixtures gently to combine.

Place 1 color in a pastry bag fitted with a ½ inch plain piping tip and pipe 12 rounds, 1¼ inches in diameter, onto 1 baking sheet. Tap the baking sheet firmly to smooth the surfaces of the macaroons. Wash and dry the bag and piping tip and pipe 12 rounds in the second color onto the other baking sheet. Allow to stand for 30 minutes.

Bake in a preheated oven, 325°F, for about 15 minutes, or until just the surfaces feel crisp. Allow to cool on the paper then carefully peel away.

rich chocolate macaroons

Makes **12**
Preparation time **20 minutes**,
  plus standing and cooling
Cooking time **20 minutes**

½ cup **confectioners' sugar**
5 tablespoons **ground almonds**
4 tablespoons **unsweetened cocoa powder**
2 **egg whites**
½ cup **superfine sugar**

Filling
5 tablespoons **heavy cream**
½ cup chopped **bittersweet chocolate**

Grease and line 2 baking sheets with nonstick parchment paper. Put the confectioners' sugar in a food processor with the ground almonds and cocoa powder and blend to a very fine consistency.

Put the egg whites in a thoroughly clean bowl and beat until peaking. Gradually beat in the superfine sugar, a tablespoonful at a time and beating well after each addition, until thick and very glossy. Add the almond mixture to the bowl and gently stir the ingredients together to combine.

Place in a pastry bag fitted with a ½ inch plain piping tip and pipe 1¼ inch rounds onto the baking sheets. Tap the baking sheet firmly to smooth the surfaces of the macaroons slightly, then allow to stand for 30 minutes. Bake in a preheated oven, 325°F, for about 15 minutes or until the surfaces feel crisp. Allow to cool before carefully peeling away the paper.

Heat the cream in a small saucepan until bubbling up around the edges but not boiling. Remove from the heat and stir in the chopped chocolate. Allow the chocolate to melt, stirring frequently, until smooth. Once the chocolate is cool and thickened enough to hold its shape, use to sandwich the macaroons together in pairs. Keep in a cool place until ready to serve.

For chocolate raspberry ganache, to serve with the macaroons, melt 3 ½ oz chocolate (see page 15) with 5 tablespoons double cream. Add 1 tablespoon unsalted butter and 3 ½ oz fresh raspberries. Heat gently over a low heat, stirring until the butter is melted. Let stand at room temperature until cool and thickened.

almond & white chocolate kisses

Makes **18**
Preparation time **25 minutes**,
  plus cooling
Cooking time **15 minutes**

²/₃ cup **blanched almonds**
½ cup **unsalted butter**,
  softened, plus extra for
  greasing
½ cup **superfine sugar**
½ cup **all-purpose flour**, plus
  extra for dusting
½ cup **self-rising flour**

Filling
½ cup chopped **white
  chocolate**
2 tablespoons **unsalted butter**

Grease 2 baking sheets.

Put the almonds in a food processor and blend until finely ground. Add the butter and sugar, sift in the flours, and blend until the mixture starts to come together.

Turn out onto a lightly floured surface and pat into a smooth dough. Roll 36 small balls of the dough, about the size of a cherry, and space on the baking sheets.

Bake in a preheated oven, 350°F, for about 15 minutes until risen, cracked, and pale golden. Transfer to a wire rack to cool.

Make the chocolate filling by melting the chocolate and butter in a saucepan. Use to sandwich the macaroons together in pairs.

For gluten-free almond macaroons, grease and line a large baking sheet with nonstick parchment paper. Beat 2 egg whites until peaking and gradually beat in ½ cup superfine sugar. Stir in 1 cup ground almonds. Place small dessertspoonfuls, spaced slightly apart, on the baking sheet and press a blanched almond onto the top of each. Bake as above.

frosted chocolate whoopies

Makes **12–14**

Preparation time **20 minutes**,
plus cooling

Cooking time **15 minutes**

butter, for greasing

1 ¼ cups **self-rising flour**

¼ teaspoon **baking soda**

¼ cup **unsweetened cocoa powder**

½ cup **superfine sugar**

2 tablespoons **vanilla sugar** (see page 168)

1 **egg**

3 tablespoons **vegetable oil**

1 tablespoon **milk**

Filling

6 tablespoons **cream cheese**

2 tablespoons **confectioners' sugar**, sifted

1 teaspoon finely grated **orange zest**

few drops of **orange extract** (optional)

Grease a large baking sheet. Put the flour, baking soda, cocoa powder, and sugars in a bowl. Beat the egg with the vegetable oil and milk and add to the dry ingredients. Beat together to form a thick paste, adding a little more milk if the mixture feels crumbly.

Take teaspoonfuls of the mixture and roll into balls, about the size of a cherry, using floured hands. Space well apart on the baking sheet and flatten slightly.

Bake in a preheated oven, 400°F, for 12 minutes until the mixture has spread and is pale golden. Transfer to a wire rack to cool.

Make the frosting by beating together the cream cheese, confectioners' sugar, orange zest, and extract, if using. Use to sandwich the cakes together. Melt the chocolate (see page 14) and spread over the tops of the whoopies.

For mascarpone and ginger frosting, to use as an alternative, finely chop 1 piece of drained stem ginger from a jar. Beat 3½ oz mascarpone cheese in a bowl with ½ oz softened unsalted butter and 3 tablespoons golden icing sugar. Stir in the ginger until evenly mixed and use to sandwich the whoopies together. Spread the tops with melted white chocolate instead of the plain or milk.

vanilla & peanut whoopies

Makes **12–14**
Preparation time **20 minutes**,
  plus cooling
Cooking time **12 minutes**

butter, for greasing
1 ½ cups **self-rising flour**,
  sifted
¼ teaspoon **baking soda**
½ cup **superfine sugar**
2 tablespoons **vanilla sugar**
  (see page 168)
1 **egg**
3 tablespoons **vegetable oil**
1 tablespoon **milk**
½ cup chopped **bittersweet
  or mik chocolate**

Filling
5 tablespoons **smooth peanut
  butter**
2 tablespoons **lightly salted
  butter**, softened
3 tablespoons **confectioners'
  sugar**, sifted
1 teaspoon **hot water**

Grease a large baking sheet.

Put the flour, baking soda, and sugars in a bowl. Beat the egg with the vegetable oil and milk and add to the bowl. Beat together to form a thick paste. Take teaspoonfuls of the mixture and roll into balls, about the size of a cherry, using floured hands. Space well apart on the baking sheet and flatten slightly.

Bake at 400°F for 12 minutes until the mixture has spread and is pale golden. Transfer to a wire rack to cool.

Make the filling by beating together the peanut butter, butter, and confectioners' sugar until smooth. Add the measurement hot water and beat until light and fluffy. Use to sandwich the cakes together.

For spiced whoopies with brandy butter, make the whoopies as above, adding 1 teaspoon ground mixed spice with the flour. Beat 75g (3 oz) softenend unsalted butter in a bowl with 25g (1oz) icing sugar and 3 tablespoons brandy until smooth and creamy. Use to sandwich the whoopies together and serve dusted with icing sugar.

scones & other mini cakes

lavender tea scones

Makes **24**

Preparation time **20 minutes**, plus cooling

Cooking time **10 minutes**

3 tablespoons chilled **unsalted butter**, diced, plus extra for greasing

2 cups **self-rising flour**, plus extra for dusting

1 teaspoon **baking powder**

4 **lavender flower stems**

2/3 cup **buttermilk**

milk or beaten **egg**, to glaze

superfine sugar, for dusting

Filling

2/3 cup **heavy cream**

4 tablespoons **strawberry jelly**

Grease a baking sheet.

Sift the flour and baking powder into a food processor. Pull the lavender flowers from the stems and add to the bowl with the butter. Blend until the mixture resembles bread crumbs. Add the buttermilk and blend briefly to make a soft dough.

Turn out onto a lightly floured surface and roll out to ³/4 inch thick. Cut out 24 rounds using a 1 ¼ inch round cutter, rerolling the trimmings as necessary. Transfer to the baking sheet, brush with milk or beaten egg, and sprinkle with superfine sugar.

Bake in a preheated oven, 425°F, for 8–10 minutes until risen and pale golden. Transfer to a wire rack to cool.

Whip the cream until just holding its shape. Split the scones and sandwich with the jelly and whipped cream.

For cranberry & orange scones, chop ¹/2 cup dried cranberries into small pieces and steep in 2 tablespoons orange juice until the orange is absorbed. Make the scones as above, adding ¼ teaspoon ground pumpkin pie spice with the flour and the cranberries and the finely grated zest of 1 small orange with the milk. Serve warm, split and buttered.

open saffron & blueberry scones

Makes **32**

Preparation time **15 minutes**, plus cooling

Cooking time **10 minutes**

3 tablespoons chilled **unsalted butter**, diced, plus extra for greasing

about ²/₃ cup **milk**

½ teaspoon **saffron strands**

2 cups **self-rising flour**, plus extra for dusting

1 teaspoon **baking powder**

1 cup **clotted cream**

1 cup **blueberries**

vanilla sugar (see page 168), to sprinkle

Grease a baking sheet.

Heat half the milk in a small saucepan. Crumble in the saffron strands and remove from the heat. Allow to cool.

Sift the flour and baking powder into a food processor and add the butter. Blend until the mixture resembles bread crumbs. Add the saffron milk and most of the remaining milk and blend briefly to make a dough, adding a little more milk if the dough feels dry.

Turn out onto a lightly floured surface and roll out to ¾ inch thick. Cut into 16 squares using a 1¼ inch cutter and place on the baking sheet.

Bake in a preheated oven, 425°F, for 8–10 minutes until risen and pale golden. Transfer to a wire rack to cool.

Split the scones in half and spread the cut sides with clotted cream. Pile the blueberries on top and serve sprinkled with vanilla sugar.

For white chocolate scones with ginger butter, make the scones as above, omitting the saffron and stirring in ¼ cup grated white chocolate before the milk. Bake as above. Chop a piece of preserved stem ginger in syrup and blend in a food processor with ⅓ cup softened unsalted butter until smooth. Blend in ¼ cup sifted confectioners' sugar and turn into a small dish. Serve with the scones.

sweet carrot & rosemary scones

Makes **22–24**
Preparation time **15 minutes**,
  plus cooling
Cooking time **10 minutes**

¼ cup chilled **lightly salted
butter**, diced, plus extra for
greasing
1 ⅓ cups **stoneground spelt
flour**, plus extra for dusting
2 teaspoons **baking powder**
½ teaspoon **cream of tartar**
2 teaspoons finely chopped
  rosemary
2 tablespoons **superfine
sugar**
1 ¼ cups finely grated small
  carrots
6 tablespoons **milk**, plus extra
to glaze

To serve
mascarpone cheese
fruit jelly, such as **crab apple**,
  apple, or **orange**

Grease a baking sheet.

Sift the flour, baking powder, and cream of tartar into
a food processor, tipping in the grains left in the sifter.
Stir in the rosemary and sugar. Add the butter and blend
until the mixture resembles bread crumbs. Stir in the
grated carrots and milk and mix to a soft dough, adding
a dash more milk if the dough feels dry.

Turn out onto a lightly floured surface and roll out to ¾
inch thick. Cut out 22–24 rounds with a 1 ¼ inch cutter,
rerolling the trimmings as necessary. Transfer to the
baking sheet and brush with beaten egg or milk
to glaze.

Bake in a preheated oven, 425°F, for 8–10 minutes
until risen and pale golden. Transfer to a wire rack
to cool.

Split the scones and serve spread with mascarpone
and fruit jelly.

For whole-wheat apple & golden raisin scones,
mix ⅔ cup whole-wheat flour, 1 cup self-rising flour, 1
teaspoon ground pumpkin pie spice, and 2 teaspoons
baking powder in a bowl. Add 3 tablespoons salted
butter, cut into small pieces, and blend with the
fingertips until the mixture resembles bread crumbs. Stir
in ⅓ cup golden raisins, chopped, and 1 peeled, cored,
and grated dessert apple. Stir in ½ cup milk and mix to
a soft dough, adding a little more milk it the dough feels
dry. Roll out, shape, and bake as above.

chocolate iced fancies

Makes **16**
Preparation time **45 minutes**,
plus cooling
Cooking time **25 minutes**

½ cup **lightly salted butter**,
softened, plus extra for
greasing
½ cup chopped **bittersweet
chocolate**
½ cup **light brown sugar**
2 **eggs**
½ cup **self-rising flour**
¼ cup **unsweetened cocoa
powder**
½ cup **ground almonds**
5 tablespoons **chocolate
hazelnut spread**

Frosting
7 oz **bittersweet chocolate**,
chopped
2 tablespoons **corn syrup**
1 tablespoon **lightly salted
butter**
¼ cup chopped **milk
chocolate**

Grease and line a 6 inch square pan with nonstick
parchment paper. Grease the paper.

Melt the chocolate (see page 14). Beat together
the butter and sugar in a bowl until pale and creamy.
Gradually beat in the eggs, adding a little flour to prevent
the mixture curdling. Stir in the melted chocolate.

Sift the flour and cocoa powder over the bowl. Add the
ground almonds and stir in gently. Turn into the pan and
level the surface. Bake in a preheated oven, 325°F, for
about 20 minutes until risen and just firm to the touch.
Transfer to a wire rack to cool.

Cut the cake into 16 squares and, using a spatula, spread
a little mound of chocolate hazelnut spread on the top of
each one. Make the frosting by melting the bittersweet
chocolate with the syrup and butter until smooth and
glossy. Separately melt the milk chocolate. Spoon a little
of the bittersweet chocolate mixture over each cake and
spread around the sides with a spatula. Using a teaspoon,
drizzle lines of milk chocolate over each cake.

For white chocolate fancies, make, bake, and cut the
cake as above, using melted white chocolate instead of
dark chocolate and adding an extra ¼ cup self-rising
flour to replace the cocoa powder. Use white chocolate
spread instead of the chocolate hazelnut spread. Make
the chocolate covering, using white chocolate instead of
the bittersweet, and use it to cover the cakes. Beat ½
cup sifted confectioners' sugar in a bowl with just enough
water to give a consistency that thickly coats the back of
the spoon. Add a drop of pink food coloring. Drizzle lines
over the cakes.

sweet potato mini loaves

Makes **10**
Preparation time **20 minutes**,
  plus cooling
Cooking time about **35
  minutes**

⅓ cup **lightly salted butter**,
  softened, plus extra for
  greasing
1 cup scrubbed and diced
  sweet potato
⅓ cup **light brown sugar**
1 teaspoon **vanilla extract**
1 **egg**
1¼ cups **self-rising flour**,
  sifted
½ teaspoon **ground
  cinnamon**
½ teaspoon **baking powder**
4 tablespoons **slivered
  almonds**, lightly crushed
¼ cup chopped **white
  chocolate**

Grease 10 mini loaf pans or sections of a linked loaf pan, each with a capacity of about ¼ cup. Stand the mini loaf pans, if using, on a baking sheet.

Cook the sweet potato in a small saucepan of boiling water for 10–15 minutes until just tender. Drain and mash. Allow to cool.

Put the butter, sugar, vanilla extract, egg, and sweet potato in a bowl, sift in the flour, cinnamon, and baking powder, and beat with a hand-held electric mixer, beat together until smooth and creamy. Divide between the pans and place on a baking sheet. Sprinkle with the slivered almonds.

Bake in a preheated oven, 325°F, for about 20 minutes until just firm to the touch. Leave in the pans for 5 minutes, then transfer to a wire rack to cool.

Melt the white chocolate (see page 14) and spoon over the tops of the cakes.

For parsnip, ginger, & hazelnut cakes, cook and mash 6 oz parsnips. Make the cake batter as above, using the parsnip mash instead of the sweet potato mash and using 1 teaspoon ground ginger instead of the cinnamon. Before baking, sprinkle with 3 tablespoons chopped hazelnuts.

honeyed fig cakes

Makes **10**
Preparation time **20 minutes**
Cooking time **15 minutes**

½ cup **lightly salted butter**,
  softened, plus extra for
  greasing
½ cup **superfine sugar**
2 **eggs**
1 cup **ground almonds**
½ teaspoon **almond extract**
¼ cup **self-rising flour**, sifted
finely grated zest of 1 **lemon**
3 **figs**, quartered
3 tablespoons **honey**
1½ tablespoons **lemon juice**

Grease and line the bases of 10 dariole molds, each with ½ cup capacity, with circles of waxed paper and stand them on a baking sheet.

Put the butter, sugar, eggs, ground almonds, almond extract, flour, and lemon zest in a bowl and beat with a hand-held electric whisk until smooth and creamy. Divide between the dariole molds. Rest a fig quarter on the center of each.

Bake in a preheated oven, 400°F, for about 15 minutes until the cake is just firm. Allow to cool in the dishes, then loosen the edges and transfer to a plate.

Mix together the honey and lemon juice and spoon over the figs.

For prune & walnut cups, grind ⅔ cup walnut pieces in a food processor or blender until finely ground. Make the cake batter as above, using the ground walnuts to replace the ground almonds and adding ⅓ cup finely chopped prunes. Bake as above and serve topped with clotted cream and a drizzle of the honey and lemon juice.

strawberry rose shortcakes

Makes **12**

Preparation time **25 minutes**, plus cooling

Cooking time **22 minutes**

½ cup **lightly salted butter**, softened, plus extra for greasing

¼ cup **superfine sugar**

1 **egg**, beaten

1 teaspoon **vanilla extract**

1 cup **self-rising flour**

½ teaspoon **baking powder**

Topping

3 tablespoons **red currant jelly**

2 teaspoons **water**

⅔ cup **heavy cream**

1 tablespoon **confectioners' sugar**, sifted

4 teaspoons **rose water**

1 cup small **strawberries**, halved

Grease 12 mini brioche molds each with a capacity of about 3 tablespoons and stand them on a baking sheet.

Cream together the butter and superfine sugar until light and fluffy. Gradually beat in the egg and vanilla extract, adding a little flour to prevent the mixture curdling. Sift the flour and baking powder into the bowl and stir in gently. Divide between the molds and level the surfaces.

Bake in a preheated oven, 350°F, for 20 minutes until just firm to the touch. Leave for 5 minutes, then tap out onto a wire rack to cool.

Make the topping by putting the red currant jelly in a small saucepan with the measurement water and heating gently until the jelly has dissolved. Turn into a small dish. Whip the cream with the confectioners' sugar and rose water until just holding its shape. Spoon on top of the shortcakes and decorate with strawberry halves. Drizzle with the red currant syrup.

For black currant cassis shortcakes, make the shortcake mixture as above, adding ¼ teaspoon ground pumpkin pie spice to the mixture. Divide between mini muffin or tartlet pans, each hole with a capacity of about 3 tablespoons. Bake as above. Invert onto a plate, skewer several holes into the center of each and spoon over 1 teaspoon of cassis liqueur so it seeps into the shortcake. Whip ⅔ cup heavy cream with 2 tablespoons sifted confectioners' sugar and pipe onto the shortcakes. Arrange a cluster of black currants on top of each and spoon over a little warmed and strained black currant jelly.

banana flapjack bites

Makes **16**
Preparation time **20 minutes**,
plus cooling
Cooking time **15 minutes**

½ cup **lightly salted butter**
¼ cup **corn syrup**
2 tablespoons **light brown
sugar**
2 cups **rolled oats**
1 ripe **banana**
1 teaspoon **lemon** or **lime
juice**
⅔ cup **heavy cream**
maple syrup, to drizzle

Place 16 mini silicone muffin cups on a baking sheet.

Put the butter, syrup, and sugar in a small saucepan and heat gently until the butter has melted. Stir in the oats until combined. Divide the mixture between the muffin cups and pack down gently with the back of a dampened teaspoon.

Bake in a preheated oven, 350°F, for 12 minutes, or until just beginning to brown around the edges. Leave in the cups for 10 minutes, then transfer to a wire rack to cool.

Mash the banana with the lemon or lime juice until pureed. Press the purée through a sieve into a bowl, scraping off the puree that clings to the underside of the sieve. Add the cream and beat until the mixture holds its shape.

Spoon the banana cream over the cakes. Drizzle with a little maple syrup just before serving.

For coconut & ginger bites, make the mixture as above, replacing ½ cup of the oats with ¾ cup shredded coconut and adding 1 finely chopped piece of preserved stem ginger in syrup. After baking, whip ⅔ cup heavy cream with 2 tablespoons of the ginger syrup. Spoon onto the cakes and decorate with coconut shavings.

bite-size vanilla sponge cakes

Makes **10**
Preparation time **20 minutes**,
  plus cooling
Cooking time **15 minutes**

⅓ cup **lightly salted butter**,
  softened
⅓ cup **superfine sugar**
¾ cup **self-rising flour**, sifted
1 **egg**, plus 1 **egg yolk**
1 teaspoon **vanilla bean
  paste**
confectioners' sugar, for
  dusting

Filling
⅔ cup **heavy cream**
5 tablespoons **strawberry** or
  raspberry jelly

Put the butter, sugar, flour, egg, egg yolk, and vanilla bean paste in a bowl and beat with a hand-held electric mixer until light and creamy. Divide between 10 holes of a mini muffin pan (greased and base-lined if not silicone).

Bake in a preheated oven, 350°F, for about 15 minutes until risen and just firm. Leave in the pan for 5 minutes, then transfer to a wire rack to cool.

Split the cakes in half horizontally. Whip the cream until just holding its shape. Use the jelly and cream to sandwich the cakes together. Serve dusted with confectioners' sugar.

For poppy seed & orange splits, make the cake batter as above, adding 1 tablespoon poppy seeds and the finely grated zest of 1 orange. Split the cakes in half horizontally and sandwich together with 5 tablespoons orange curd. Blend ¾ cup sifted confectioners' sugar with about 2 teaspoons orange juice to give a consistency that thickly coats the back of the spoon. Gently spread the icing over the tops of the cakes.

lemon glazed cardamom madeleines

Makes about **30**
Preparation time **20 minutes**,
plus setting
Cooking time **30 minutes**

½ cup **lightly salted butter**,
melted, plus extra for
greasing
1 cup **self-rising flour**, plus
extra for dusting
2 teaspoons **cardamom pods**
3 **eggs**
½ cup **superfine sugar**
finely grated zest of 1 **lemon**
½ teaspoon **baking powder**

Glaze
2 tablespoons **lemon juice**
¾ cup **confectioners' sugar**,
sifted, plus extra for dusting

Grease a madeleine sheet with melted butter and dust with flour. Tap out the excess flour.

Crush the cardamom pods using a mortar and pestle to release the seeds. Remove the shells and crush the seeds a little more.

Put the eggs, superfine sugar, lemon zest, and crushed cardamom seeds in a heatproof bowl and rest the bowl over a saucepan of gently simmering water. Beat with a hand-held electric mixer until the mixture is thick and pale and the mixer leaves a trail when lifted.

Sift the flour and baking powder into the bowl and gently fold in using a large metal spoon. Drizzle the melted butter around the edges of the mixture and fold the ingredients together until just combined. Spoon the mixture into the madeleine sections until about two-thirds full. (Keep the remaining mixture aside for baking a second batch.) Bake in a preheated oven, 425°F, for about 10 minutes until risen and golden. Leave in the pan for 5 minutes, then transfer to a wire rack to cool.

Put the lemon juice in a bowl and beat in the confectioners' sugar. Brush over the madeleines and allow to set. Serve dusted with confectioners' sugar.

For espresso madeleines with coffee glaze, mix 1 teaspoon instant espresso coffee powder with 2 teaspoons hot water. Make the madeleines as above, adding the coffee mixture once the mix leaves a trail. Bake as above. Mix an additional ½ teaspoon espresso coffee powder with 2 teaspoons hot water. Beat with ½ cup sifted confectioners' sugar until smooth and use to brush over the madeleines.

lamingtons

Makes **24**
Preparation time **20 minutes**,
   plus overnight standing and
   setting
Cooking time **30 minutes**

½ cup **unsalted butter**,
   softened, plus extra for
   greasing
½ cup **superfine sugar**
2 **eggs**, lightly beaten
2 cups **self-rising flour**, sifted
pinch of **salt**
4 tablespoons **milk**
1 teaspoon **vanilla extract**

Coating
3 cups **confectioners' sugar**
1 cup **unsweetened cocoa
   powder**
about ¾ cup boiling **water**
2¾ cups **shredded coconut**

Grease a 7 x 10 inch cake pan and base-line with nonstick parchment paper.

Beat the butter and sugar together in a mixing bowl until pale and creamy. Gradually beat in the eggs, adding a little flour to prevent the mixture curdling. Add the flour and salt and fold in with the milk and vanilla extract. Turn into the pan and level the surface.

Bake in a preheated oven, 375°F, for 25–30 minutes until risen and firm to the touch. Allow the cake to cool in the pan for 5 minutes then loosen the edges, transfer to a wire rack and peel off the lining paper. Leave out overnight, then cut into 24 pieces.

Make the coating by sifting the confectioners' sugar and cocoa powder into a bowl, making a well in the center and beating in the boiling water to make a smooth chocolate icing with a pouring consistency. Pour the shredded coconut onto a plate.

Use 2 forks to dip each cake into the icing and then immediately coat with the coconut all over. Leave to set on nonstick parchment paper.

For cherry and almond splits, make the cake as above, adding ½ cup sour dried cherries, finely chopped, and 1 teaspoon almond extract. Once cooled, cut it in half horizontally and sandwich back together with 6 tablespoons cherry preserves, chopping any large pieces of fruit first. Sift 1¾ cups confectioners' sugar into a bowl and mix in 5–6 teaspoons cold water to make a spreadable icing. Spread over the cake and sprinkle with toasted and crushed slivered almonds. Allow to firm up for 30 minutes, then cut into squares.

treats for kids

baby butterflies

Makes **16**
Preparation time **25 minutes**,
  plus cooling
Cooking time **12 minutes**

¼ cup **lightly salted butter**,
  softened
¼ cup **superfine sugar**
½ cup **self-rising flour**, sifted
1 teaspoon **vanilla extract**
1 **egg**
confectioners' sugar, for
  dusting

Buttercream
⅓ cup **unsalted butter**,
  softened
1 cup **confectioners' sugar**,
  sifted
pink food coloring
1 teaspoon hot **water**

Place 16 mini silicone muffin cups on a baking sheet.

Put the butter, sugar, flour, vanilla extract, and egg in a bowl and beat with a hand-held electric mixer until light and creamy. Divide between the muffin cups.

Bake in a preheated oven, 350°F, for 10–12 minutes until risen and just firm. Allow to cool in the cups for 2 minutes then transfer to a wire rack to cool completely.

Make the buttercream by beating together the butter and confectioners' sugar until combined. Add a little pink food coloring and the measurement water and beat until smooth and creamy.

Use a small sharp knife to cut out circles from the tops of the cakes and cut the circles in half to shape butterfly wings. Put the buttercream in a pastry bag fitted with a small star tip and use to pipe swirls into the scooped-out tops of the cakes. Position the butterfly wings on top and dust lightly with confectioners' sugar.

For white chocolate frosting, melt ½ cup chopped white chocolate with 2 tablespoons unsalted butter in a microwave on full power for 5 minutes, removing after 2 minutes to stir thoroughly, and again after 4 minutes, to ensure no lumps remain. Sift in 1 cup confectioners' sugar. Stir well until combined. Use instead of the buttercream to spoon or pipe onto the cakes.

vanilla flowers

Makes **30**
Preparation time **30 minutes**
Cooking time **15 minutes**

1 cup **butter**, softened, plus
extra for greasing
few drops of **vanilla extract**
½ cup **confectioners' sugar**
1½ cups **all-purpose flour**
¾ cup **cornstarch**
cake decorations, to decorate

Grease and line 2 large baking sheets with nonstick parchment paper.

Place the butter and vanilla extract in a mixing bowl and sift in the confectioners' sugar. Cream the ingredients together with a wooden spoon. Sift in the flour and the cornstarch a little at a time and fold in with a metal spoon.

Place the dough in a pastry bag fitted with a ½ inch star tip and pipe onto the baking sheet, making 30 little flower shapes, spacing them slightly apart to allow room for spreading. To finish a flower, push the tip down into the piped flower as you stop squeezing. Press a decoration into the center of each one.

Bake in a preheated oven, 375°F, for 10–15 minutes, or until a pale golden color. Allow to cool for a few minutes on the baking sheets before transferring to a wire rack to cool.

For chocolate sandwiches, make the cookie dough as above and put into a pastry bag fitted with a ½ inch star tip. Pipe 3 thin lines of the dough, each touching the previous line, to shape a rectangular cookie measuring about 2 x 1¼ inches. Repeat with the remaining dough, spacing them slightly apart to allow room for spreading, making sure you end up with an even number. Bake as above. Melt 3 oz milk chocolate (see page 14) and use to sandwich the cookies together.

candy-topped cookie cakes

Makes **16**
Preparation time **15 minutes**,
  plus cooling
Cooking time **12 minutes**

¼ cup **unsalted butter**
2 tablespoons **corn syrup**
1 cup **rolled oats**
⅔ cup **shredded coconut**
⅓ cup **dried cranberries**,
  chopped
½ cup **confectioners' sugar**,
  sifted
1½ teaspoons **water**
**mini sugar-coated chocolate
  beans**, to decorate

Place 16 mini silicone muffin cups on a baking sheet.

Put the butter and syrup in a small saucepan and heat gently until the butter has melted. Remove from the heat and stir in the rolled oats, coconut, and cranberries. Beat well until evenly mixed, then turn into the muffin cups and pack down gently.

Bake in a preheated oven, 375°F, for about 12 minutes, or until turning golden around the edges. Allow to cool in the cups.

Beat the confectioners' sugar with the measurement water and drizzle a little around the edges of the cakes. Gently press the chocolate beans into the icing.

For tangy yogurt frosting, line a strainer with 4 thicknesses of paper towel and spoon 6 tablespoons plain whole milk yogurt into the strainer. Bring up the edges of the paper and gently squeeze out the liquid from the yogurt until you have a thickened ball of yogurt. Tip into a bowl with 1 cup sifted confectioners' sugar and mix to form a soft frosting. Swirl over the cakes instead of using the icing and candies.

chocolate kittens

Makes **20**

Preparation time **1 hour**, plus chilling

Cooking time **15 minutes**

butter, for greasing

1 quantity **chocolate sable dough** (made by substituting ¼ cup flour with unsweetened cocoa powder in the vanilla sable dough, page 76)

flour, for dusting

6 oz **pink rolled fondant**

edible silver or **gold dragees**

2 oz **pale brown rolled fondant**

6 oz **blue rolled fondant**

6 oz **chocolate-flavored rolled fondant**

1 **tube black decorator frosting**

Buttercream

¾ cup **confectioners' sugar**, plus extra for dusting

¼ cup **lightly salted butter**, softened

½ teaspoon hot **water**

Grease a large baking sheet.

Roll out the cookie dough on a lightly floured surface and cut out rounds using a 3¼ inch cookie cutter, rerolling the trimmings to make 20 in all. Place on the baking sheet, spacing them slightly apart.

Bake in a preheated oven, 350°F, for 15 minutes, or until beginning to darken around the edges. Transfer to a wire rack to cool.

Make the buttercream by beating together the confectioners' sugar, butter, and measurement water until smooth and creamy. Put the buttercream in a pastry bag fitted with a fine plain tip.

Make the kittens by shaping 10 triangular pieces of pink fondant for noses on a sugar-dusted surface. Secure to the centers of half the cookies with buttercream. Press 1¾ inch strips of pink fondant to the base of the cookies. Stud with silver or gold dragees to make collars. Shape pointed ears in pale brown fondant and secure with buttercream. Pipe features onto the faces with the buttercream, then add round eyes and bow ties made of blue fondant. With the decorator frosting, draw a black line down the center of the eyes.

For chocolate puppies, shape 10 triangles of pale brown fondant for noses. Secure to the centers of the remaining cookies with buttercream. Make collars in blue fondant. Pipe features with buttercream, then add ears, pink tongues, and brown eyes.

magic wands

Makes **14**
Preparation time **25 minutes**,
  plus setting
Cooking time **15 minutes**

1 cup **unsalted butter**,
  softened, plus extra for
  greasing
¼ cup **superfine sugar**
2 cups **all-purpose flour**,
  sifted
1 teaspoon **vanilla extract**
a few drops each of **yellow**
  and **orange liquid food
  coloring**
1¼ cups **royal icing sugar**,
  sifted
**different-colored sugar
  sprinkles**
edible silver dragees

Grease 2 baking sheets. Beat together the butter and sugar until very pale and creamy. Beat in the flour and vanilla extract until smooth.

Divide the cookie dough in half and stir the yellow food coloring into one half and the orange coloring into the other. Put the cookie dough into 2 large pastry bags fitted with ½ inch plain tips. Pipe fingers onto the baking sheets, each about 5 inches long, spacing them slightly apart.

Bake in a preheated oven, 350°F, for 15 minutes, or until slightly risen and just beginning to darken. Allow to cool for 5 minutes, then transfer to a wire rack to cool completely.

Beat the royal icing sugar with enough water to give a consistency that just holds its shape. Spread a little icing over one end of each cookie and sprinkle with plenty of sugar sprinkles and silver dragees. Leave in a cool place to set for about 1 hour.

For fun letter cookies, make the cookie dough as above, but without adding the food coloring. Place in a pastry bag fitted with a ¼ inch plain tip. Use to pipe letter shapes, about 2 inches tall, onto the baking sheets. Bake as above. Decorate with tubes of colorful decorator frosting, securing small candies or sugar sprinkles.

sticky chocolate orange cakes

Makes **16**
Preparation time **20 minutes**
Cooking time **15 minutes**

¼ cup **lightly salted butter**, softened
¼ cup **superfine sugar**
½ cup **self-rising flour**, sifted
finely grated zest of ½ **orange**
1 **egg**
6 tablespoons **orange jelly marmalade**
2 teaspoons **water**
6 tablespoons **chopped milk chocolate**

Place 16 mini silicone muffin cups on a baking sheet.

Put the butter, sugar, flour, orange zest, and egg in a bowl and beat with a hand-held electric mixer until light and creamy. Divide between the muffin cups.

Bake in a preheated oven, 350°F, for 10–12 minutes until risen and just firm. allow to cool in the cups for 2 minutes before transferring to a wire rack to cool completely.

Use a teaspoon to scoop out (and discard) a little from the top of each cake to make a small cavity. Put the marmalade in a small saucepan with the measurement water and heat gently until the marmalade has melted. Allow to cool slightly, then spoon a little onto the top of each cake. Allow to set.

Melt the chocolate (see page 14). Spoon onto the tops of the cakes and spread gently to the edges.

For teatime strawberry cakes, make the cakes as above, omitting the orange zest and adding 1 teaspoon vanilla extract. After baking, remove the cakes from the muffin cups and split in half horizontally. Sandwich each back together with 1 teaspoon strawberry-flavored yogurt and a thin slice of strawberry. Dust the tops with confectioners' sugar.

wiggly worm

Serves **11**

Preparation time **45 minutes**, plus cooling

Cooking time **20 minutes**

²/₃ cup **lightly salted butter**, softened

²/₃ cup **superfine sugar**

1½ cups **self-rising flour**, sifted

3 **eggs**

1 teaspoon **vanilla extract**

¼ cup grated **milk chocolate**

confectioners' sugar, for dusting

3 ½ oz **pink** or **red rolled fondant**

2 oz **chocolate-flavored rolled fondant**

12 small **sugar-covered chocolate candies**

Buttercream

⅓ cup **unsalted butter**, softened

1 cup **confectioners' sugar**, sifted

Line a 12-hole cupcake pan with paper bake cups. Put the butter, sugar, flour, eggs, and vanilla extract in a bowl and beat with a hand-held electric mixer until smooth and creamy. Divide the mixture between the paper cups. Bake in a preheated oven, 350°F, for 20 minutes or until risen and just firm to the touch. Transfer to a wire rack to cool.

Make the buttercream by beating together the butter and sugar in a bowl until smooth and creamy. Remove one cooled cake from its cup and take a thick, angled slice off the top, and discard. Spread a little of the buttercream over another cake, position the slice on top, and spread with a little more buttercream to make a large face.

Spread a large, rectangular board with 4 tablespoons of the buttercream and sprinkle with the grated chocolate. Spread the remaining buttercream over the cakes, then position in a snaking line over the chocolate, with the face cake at the front.

Roll out the pink or red fondant thinly on a surface lightly dusted with confectioners' sugar and cut out 9 rounds using a 2 inch cookie cutter. Place on all the cakes except the face and end cakes. Cut out a pointed tail from the trimmings and place on the end cake.

Roll out the chocolate fondant and cut out a round using a slightly larger cutter. Position on the face cake. Then cut out ten 1 inch rounds. Place on the rest of the cakes and top each with a sugar-covered chocolate candy. Shape and position some eyes and a mouth using the fondant trimmings and remaining candies.

birthday cake stack

Makes **18**

Preparation time **25 minutes**, plus cooling

Cooking time **20 minutes**

¾ cup **lightly salted butter**, softened

¾ cup **superfine sugar**

3 **eggs**

1¾ cups **self-rising flour**

1 teaspoon **baking powder**

finely grated zest of 2 **lemons**

To decorate

½ cup **unsalted butter**, softened

1¾ cups **confectioners' sugar**, sifted

a few drops of **pink** or **blue food coloring**

4 oz **small candies**, such as dolly mixtures and gummy candies

sugar sprinkles (optional)

birthday candles and **candleholders**

Line 18 holes of 2 x 12-hole muffin pans with paper bake cups. Put the butter, superfine sugar, eggs, flour, baking powder, and lemon zest in a bowl and beat with a hand-held electric mixer for about 1 minute until light and creamy. Divide the batter between the paper cups.

Bake in a preheated oven, 350°F, for 20 minutes, until risen and just firm to touch. Transfer to a wire rack.

Make the buttercream by beating together the unsalted butter and confectioners' sugar in a bowl until smooth and creamy. Beat in the food coloring. Spread the buttercream over the cooled cakes using a small spatula. Decorate the cakes with plenty of small candies and sugar sprinkles, if using.

Arrange a layer of cakes on a serving plate and stack another 2 or 3 tiers on top. Push the required amount of birthday candles and candleholders into the cakes.

For christmas cake stack, make the cakes as above, using red, white, or silver paper cups or a mixture of all three. Beat ⅓ cup soft unsalted butter with 1 cup sifted confectioners' sugar until light and fluffy, then spread over the cakes. Thinly roll out 5 oz white rolled fondant on a surface dusted with confectioners' sugar and cut out rounds using a 2½ inch cutter. Position on top of the cakes. Roll out the white fondant trimmings and 2 oz red rolled fondant and cut out star shapes in various sizes in both colors. Allow to set on nonstick parchment paper, then arrange over the stacked cakes along with small candy canes and silver dragees, secured to the white fondant with dots of decorator frosting.

milk chocolate crackles

Makes **16**
Preparation time **10 minutes**,
plus setting

7 oz **milk chocolate**, chopped
5 cups **corn flakes**
colored sugar sprinkles, to
decorate

Place 16 mini silicone muffin cups on a tray.

Melt the chocolate (see page 14). Using your hands,
crush the corn flakes until broken into very small flakes.
Tip into the chocolate and mix thoroughly until the corn
flakes are coated in a thin film of chocolate.

Use a teaspoon to scoop the mixture into the muffin
cups, packing it down firmly so the cakes will hold
together when set. Decorate with sugar sprinkles.
Chill for about 1 hour until set.

For chocolate refrigerator cakes, melt 5 oz milk
chocolate in a pan with 2 tablespoons unsalted butter,
stirring frequently until the mixture is smooth. Cut 4
marshmallows into small pieces with scissors and chop
4 shortbread cookies or graham crackers into pieces no
bigger than ½ inch. Roughly chop 8 candied cherries.
Add to the bowl and mix until coated in chocolate.
Divide between 16 mini silicone muffin cups and
sprinkle with white chocolate shavings. Chill as above.

happy faces

Makes **16**
Preparation time **40 minutes**,
plus chilling
Cooking time **15 minutes**

½ lb (2 sticks) chilled **unsalted butter**, cut into pieces, plus extra for greasing
2¼ cups **all-purpose flour**, plus extra for dusting
1 cup **confectioners' sugar**, sifted
2 **egg yolks**
2 teaspoons **vanilla bean paste**
4 tablespoons **strawberry** or **raspberry jelly**

Buttercream
1 cup **confectioners' sugar**
⅓ cup **unsalted butter**, softened
1 teaspoon hot **water**

Grease 2 baking sheets.

Put the butter and flour in a food processor and blend until the mixture resembles bread crumbs. Add the sugar, egg yolks, and vanilla and blend until the mixture comes together to form a smooth dough. Wrap in plastic wrap and chill for at least 1 hour.

Roll out the cookie dough on a lightly floured surface. Cut out rounds using a 2½ inch cookie cutter, rerolling the trimmings to make 32 in all. Place on the baking sheets, spaced slightly apart.

Cut out eyes in half the rounds, using a ½ inch cookie cutter or the end of a large, plain piping tip. Also cut out a large, smiling mouth, using a small, sharp knife or craft knife. Bake in a preheated oven, 350°F, for 15 minutes, or until pale golden, then transfer to a wire rack to cool.

Make the buttercream by beating together the confectioners' sugar, butter, and measurement water until smooth and creamy. Spread the buttercream over the plain cookies, then spread with the jelly. Gently press the face cookies on top.

For chocolate heart cookies, make the dough as above, replacing 3 tablespoons of the flour with unsweetened cocoa powder. Cut out heart shapes from half the cookies using a small cutter and bake as above. Once cooled, sandwich the cookies together in pairs with white chocolate spread. Melt 2 oz white chocolate and spoon into the corner of a small plastic bag. Snip off the merest tip and pipe an outline around the edges of the hearts.

little dinos

Makes **20**
Preparation time **1 hour**, plus chilling
Cooking time **15 minutes**

½ lb (2 sticks) chilled **unsalted butter**, diced, plus extra for greasing

2¼ cups **all-purpose flour**, plus extra for dusting

1 cup **confectioners' sugar**, plus extra for dusting

2 **egg yolks**

2 teaspoons **vanilla bean paste**

10 oz **green rolled fondant**

4 oz **yellow rolled fondant**

2¾ oz **white chocolate rainbow buttons**

1 oz **brown rolled fondant**

Buttercream

1 cup **confectioners' sugar**, sifted

⅓ cup **unsalted butter**, softened

1 teaspoon hot **water**

Grease 2 baking sheets. Put the butter and flour in a food processor and blend until the mixture resembles bread crumbs. Add the sugar, egg yolks, and vanilla and blend until the mixture comes together as a smooth dough. Wrap in plastic wrap and chill for 1 hour.

Roll out the cookie dough on a lightly floured surface and cut out rounds with a 4 inch cutter, rerolling the trimmings to make 40 in all. Cut each round in half. Place on baking sheets, spacing them slightly apart. Bake in a preheated oven, 350°F, for 15 minutes, or until pale golden. Transfer to a wire rack to cool. Knead the green fondant a little on a surface lightly dusted with confectioners' sugar. Tear the yellow fondant into bits and dot over the green fondant. Roll the lump of icing into a thick sausage. Fold it in half and roll again. Repeat the rolling and folding until the colors have marbled. Beat together the confectioners' sugar and butter with the measurement water until smooth and creamy. Roll out the marbled fondant thinly. Lay a cookie over the fondant and, using a small, sharp knife or craft knife, cut around it, adding an icing tail.

Pipe a little buttercream over the cookie and lay the marbled fondant on top. Repeat with the rest of the cookies. Reroll the fondant trimmings and cut out small heads, marking mouths with the tip of a knife. Secure to the bodies with buttercream. Shape and secure ears and feet. Cut the chocolate buttons carefully into triangular shapes and, using buttercream, secure along the top edge of each dinosaur "body," making the triangles smaller at the tail end. Pipe eyes and claws with buttercream. Shape and secure small balls of brown fondant for the centers of the eyes.

wise old owls

Makes **18**
Preparation time **1¼ hours**,
  plus setting
Cooking time **15 minutes**

butter, for greasing
1 quantity **vanilla cookie
  dough**, chilled (see page
  230)
flour, for dusting
1 tablespoon **egg white**,
  lightly beaten
2 teaspoons **unsweetened
  cocoa powder**
1 teaspoon **water**
1¼ cups **royal icing sugar**,
  sifted
2 oz each of **white, blue, and
  yellow rolled fondant**

Grease 2 baking sheets. Copy the owl picture opposite to make a template. Roll out the cookie dough on a lightly floured surface. Lay the template over the dough and, using a small, sharp knife or craft knife, cut around it. Reroll the trimmings to make 18 in all. Place on the baking sheets, spaced slightly apart.

Beat together the egg white, cocoa powder, and measurement water to make a smooth, thin paste. Using a fine paintbrush, paint the wing, head, and beak areas on the owls. Bake in a preheated oven, 350°F, for 15 minutes, or until pale golden. Using a spatula, transfer to a wire rack to cool.

Beat the royal icing sugar with enough water to give a consistency that just holds its shape. Put the royal icing in a pastry bag fitted with a fine plain tip. Use the white fondant to shape round eyes, then secure them in place with a little royal icing from the bag. Use the blue fondant to shape centers for the eyes, then secure with royal icing. Cut out feet shapes in yellow fondant and secure in place. Use the icing left in the bag to paint the wing and breast feathers. Leave in a cool place to set for about 1 hour.

For trick-or-treat ghosties, roll out the dough as above and cut out shapes using a ghost-shaped cutter. Bake as above and allow to cool. Blend 1¾ cups sifted royal icing sugar with enough water to make a paste that is spreadable but holds its shape. Using a spatula, spread the icing over the cookies. Allow to set for a couple of hours. Use a tube of black decorator frosting to pipe around eyes and smiling mouths.

window cookies

Makes **10**
Preparation time **10 minutes**,
  plus cooling
Cooking time **20 minutes**

1 quantity **Vanilla Cookie
  Dough**, chilled (see page
  230)
flour, for dusting
175g (6 oz) **coloured boiled
  sweets**, lightly crushed
1 quantity **Royal Icing** (see
  page 15)
10 **chocolate flakes**
12 small **sugar-coated
  chocolates**
sugar sprinkles, to decorate

Line 2 baking sheets with nonstick baking paper. Roll out the cookie dough on a lightly floured surface. Cut out 10 x 8 cm (4 x 3¼ inches) rectangles and transfer to the baking sheets.

Cut out 4 squares from each rectangle to resemble window panes. Gather the trimmings and reroll the dough to make more window shapes. Place the windows on the baking sheets and put a boiled sweet in each cut out square.

Bake in a preheated oven at 180°C (350°F), Gas Mark 4 for 12 minutes or until the cookies begin to colour and the sweets have melted to fill the frames. If necessary ease the sweets into the corners with a toothpick. Leave to cool on the baking sheets. Place the icing in a piping bag fitted with a fine plain nozzle. Pipe a little icing onto the back of each flake bar and secure one flake along the base of each cookie. Make sure the chocolate sits straight along the bottom so it supports the cookie.

Add flower petals and trailing leaves around the windows, using the remaining icing in the bag. Before it sets, press small candies into the frames in the centres of the windows.

Leave to cool before carefully peeling away the paper.

index

acknowledgments

Commissioning editor: Eleanor Maxfield
Editor: Joanne Wilson
Photographic Art Direction: Tracy Killick and Karen Sawyer
Designer: Karen Sawyer
Photographer: Will Heap
Home Economist: Joanna Farrow
Props Stylist: Rachel Jukes
Senior Production Controller: Lucy Carter

Special photography: © Octopus Publishing Group Limited/Will Heap **Other photography:** Octopus Publishing Group 16, 160; /Stephen Conroy 6, 14, 61, 121, 125, 159, 167; /Vanessa Davies 213; /Will Heap 4, 126, 137, 149; /William Lingwood 155; /David Munns 12 right, 33, 63, 223, 225; /Emma Neish 53, 113; /Lis Parsons 79, 87, 89, 91, 93, 95, 97, 217, 219, 229, 231, 233, 235; /William Shaw 43, 75, 83, 105, 135, 143, 145, 171, 173; /Ian Wallace 12 left, 71, 207